BELIEVING UNITY

DISCOVERING THE ONENESS OF
MIND, MATTER AND CONSCIOUSNESS

First published 2022 by Naratva Publishing

Contact:
naratvapublishing@proton.me

ISBN: 978-1-7391356-2-1

To Everyone and Everything,
I am Eternally Grateful

Content

o

INTRODUCTION

Hello and welcome, dear reader. I would like to share something of tremendous beauty with you. May this book serve as a catalyst for profound conversations, deep exploration of the nature of reality, and self-realisation. Whether it becomes an ongoing dialogue between you and your past, you and your friends or family, or between you and me, let's peacefully follow the thread of inspiration.

I feel there is nothing of more importance in life than to understand the nature of the self, of what it is to *be*. It is a marvellous and frankly utterly astonishing truth that existence *is*. The enigma of existence holds within it a sense of profound mystery, capable of expanding our consciousness with a mere moment's contemplation. This mystery surpasses the trivialities of territorial disputes and transcends the boundaries of race, gender, and species. It doesn't make any difference if you say you're a giraffe or a human, both *exist*. What *is* that?

We're told all manner of answers, likely first from our parents, then school teachers, popular media, religious organisations, sciences, and so on. Authority figures tell us who we are before we really have a chance to figure it out for ourselves. The question might then be, "Which is the correct authority?" or, "Who do I trust?" This will just lead to comparison, opposition, to differing and seemingly arbitrary standards of right and wrong, and inevitably into total war as everyone fights each other to be 'correct,' ultimately crumbling under the weight of our own self-importance. But history shows that much of what was once considered true has been later surpassed by new discoveries. Superseded by a further openness of mind, a curiosity to investigate what was taken for granted, or reconsidered to a depth that would have been previously simply unfathomable.

So actually, what is the *real* authority here? It clearly goes beyond merely listening to one particular human's opinion as gospel. We seem to be, as many philosophers have pointed out over the years, adhering to a 'higher' standard. Many have phrased this higher standard, as reason.

It's the discriminating mind that reflects, compares, contrasts, and attempts to reconcile contradictory information to find a sense of harmony. When I give you a piece of information that is in contradiction to everything else you know, your discriminating mind will naturally react to that by reawakening dormant information relating to the subject at hand. For example, did you know that *all* horses have white tails? ...

If there is not initial doubt, and for some reason I have become an authority that need not be questioned, you may simply say, "Oh, interesting" and just accept it. I'd argue you're just not paying full attention.

'Just accepting it' is not what is being asked of you when reading this book. Doubt freely, but try not to remain in doubt, *investigate* the mysteries being provoked in your mind. If you doubt, if you ask, "Do *all* horses have white tails?" you open your mind and allow it to present all the information you have pertaining to horses. In no time at all you can remember horses with brown or black tails and you could maybe even take me to a field nearby to demonstrate that. So, after reflection, my position that all horses have white tails is unreasonable. I am living with a belief that is incongruent with observation.

When I see the horses with black tails and brown tails I then have two options. I can see that I've been mistaken and incorporate this information into my outlook; or, I can continue the narrative of exclusively white tailed horses through the method of denial: "Those tails have been dyed by humans for aesthetic purposes," for example. In those moments we'd say that I wouldn't listen to reason.

Here, reason seems like a higher authority because it appears as if it's an external standard that can or 'ought' to influence the opinions of any given human.

So now I'm led to the question, what is the foundation of reason?

Is reason truly external? It seems not, because if there were no innate capacity to reflect and contrast thoughts within oneself then reason itself would be impossible. How can you give reason to something that by its nature is unreasonable and so would not be able to use the tool of reason... reasonably?

Giving a car to a mouse as a birthday gift is by all accounts unreasonable. It simply won't be able to make use of it outside of its own ideas of utility. It may take the stuffing out of the seats for a cosy nest, but embarking on a shopping trip with it is virtually impossible - unless we're dealing with a cartoon mouse. It makes use of what it is given according to its own understanding. Reason therefore is innate; it is intrinsic, whatever it is.

Now, without veering off course too much, let's take a moment to appreciate the absurdity that arises when fear assumes the captain's seat of reason. It leads us to the most peculiar conclusions that, once fear is dismissed from its post, become glaringly unreasonable: "I apologise, Captain, but it seemed perfectly logical at the time to steer the ship ashore to evade those menacing sharks!" Fear-driven decision-making, when seen without fear, shows how rationality can take an unexpected detour into the realms of the comical.

So reason is not an objective truth that exists independent of the mind but must be a function of mind. Further to this, the standard of what is reasonable can only be based on the current knowledge of the culture. I'm sure there were cultures who believed cannibalism was reasonable and by and large these cultures have died out, perhaps never even realising that eating each other was the cause until chewing their own fingers. Culture sets a standard of how information 'ought' to be processed to come to some outcome that is tending towards the maximisation of a given value or virtue.

If we take the ideology of capitalism as an example, we see that 'reasonable' business models are those that process their information tending towards a maximisation of profit as a value. A business is then valued based on its ability to maximise profit, and this is considered reasonable. In the case of a charity, processing information tending towards the maximisation of wellbeing and peace is perhaps the most reasonable. Any action or information processing that results in the destruction of wellbeing, destruction of environments and so on would be considered highly unreasonable for a charity - not so in many businesses one may observe.

Yet the foundation of reason is more than simply setting a standard, and it's more than the standard itself. There is no 'ultimate standard' of reason that should be aimed for as if one could ever be objectively better than any other. The standard can be chosen at random, but each standard has consequences. The fear of Artificial Intelligence (AI) stems from the realisation that the standards we establish may inadvertently result in actions that achieve the intended goal but ultimately lead to the destruction of humanity. It is akin to the cautionary tale of the monkey's paw, where a wish is granted, but at a great cost. For instance, consider the objective of eliminating suffering. If AI were to interpret this goal in a literal sense, it might indiscriminately eliminate all living beings, thereby achieving the goal, but bringing about the very outcome we sought to prevent.

A standard of reason exclusively centred around profit (or 'economic growth') means that the health of the environment and overall wellbeing of animals, plants and fungi will be compromised and even destroyed as a consequence. It's an ironic paradox where the pursuit of survival ultimately beckons destruction. If everyone wants to go in that direction, it's neither better nor worse than a standard of wellbeing. It's just that it means lots of misery and suffering. Again, if we want to suffer, we can just keep going that way. It's only from a goal or standard of wellbeing, happiness, and peace that one can say a continuation of suffering is unreasonable.

What is even more intriguing is that reason relies on the presence of harmony. Something becomes reasonable when it integrates multiple pieces of information and aligns with a perception of harmony within nature. On a larger scale, suffering is occasionally deemed 'justified' when it is an unintended consequence of harmonising something else perceived as more significant ("we understand you're suffering, but we're close to paying off the national debt").

Here, we encounter the concept of a 'small mind,' not in an antagonistic sense, but rather as an observational standpoint. A small mind can be described as processing information to harmonise only a limited number of factors, such as personal safety or individual gains, without considering the broader disharmony resulting from those actions.

Reason can be seen as the process of harmonising information, whereby the greater the amount of information that can be harmonised, the more 'reasonable' a statement becomes. At its highest level, reason allows for the harmonisation of seemingly contradictory statements. This can be exemplified in statements found in Zen Buddhism, like the famous, "Suchness is nothing and nothing is suchness." In this case, maximal harmony is achieved as all opposition is dissolved.

As soon as we gain a new perspective or understanding, it becomes a valuable addition to our knowledge and automatically transforms our capacity for reason. This newfound knowledge informs our decision-making process. Therefore, any form of learning expands our reasoning abilities and contributes to the overall harmony of our culture. The key is to integrate new and old information together to avoid cognitive dissonance, which perpetuates internal opposition. Reason, in this sense, is not abstract or objective but a process of equilibrium, reflecting the nature of the entire cosmos.

If there is a standard of reason worth pursuing, it is the attainment of total harmony and unity. This process is exemplified in physics, particularly in the pursuit of a Grand Unified Theory of Everything. However, in a state of total harmony, reason becomes unnecessary. At that point, there are no distinct elements that require reconciliation with the totality. Hence, the need for rationalisation diminishes and we can simply exist as we are.

When beginning such an investigation, there are two approaches. The first option involves starting from complete fragmentation and attempting to piece everything back together, like a cosmic jigsaw puzzle. The second option involves beginning afresh with reason as the tool of investigation. I have chosen the latter approach, starting from a state of no assumption of division and gradually reconciling and harmonising any distinctions and oppositions that arise as we investigate our perspective.

Every day, millions of people opt for the first approach, starting from the standpoint of duality, division, and separation. Unfortunately, this often leads to further division, as the underlying premise is that everything is fundamentally fragmented. Beginning with that assumption, how could those holding this point of view be happy with the fruits of their investigation until they find more fragments? Unity is therefore a negation of the entire endeavour. The goal is defined from the beginning as forever elusive.

So let's use the method children learn with the mazes on the back of cereal boxes. Let's start from the center, from where we want to get to, and work our way back to the outside. At the minute, the reasonable explanations function to perpetuate and solidify division, rather than dissolve it. It is the nature of the tool being used - the language. If we want to take a nail out of a plank of wood, and the only tool we have is a mallet, the best thing to do is hit the nail from the other side. So we must change our perspective here too. There can only be equality and unity if there is, in actuality, no division; otherwise, the unity is more like a magic trick, an illusion.

I invite you then, on a transformative journey, beginning at the core of philosophical experience and venturing into a fresh perspective on the physical world, the mind, and the nature of consciousness. This exploration will lead us to a new conceptual structure, a harmonious schema aligned with observation that has its nose pressed against the edge of reason, staring into the face of unity.

Serving as a radiant focal point, this schema acts as the luminous accretion disc encircling the event horizon of the infinite black hole. Its purpose is not to assert correctness, but rather to serve as a vehicle that directs attention towards something greater - the very center of the black hole. Symbolic language, words, and metaphors are employed to evoke a direct experience that transcends linguistic expression, measurement, and intellect. This schema, therefore, does not seek to impart intellectual knowledge for the sake of intellectual prowess, but rather to uncover and immerse oneself in the essence of reality - the exploration of what it truly means to exist.

This schema is adaptable. If new knowledge comes along that contradicts something within it, this schema can change to accommodate because it is working from the foundation of unity. It matters not how we divide unity, it is just interesting that it seems divided at all. The symbols and metaphors used here are of this particular time in history. In the future these symbols may seem out-dated, but in that case, the symbols can change. What is being pointed to is much more important than the structures erected around it. This book is essentially a holistic rationale, crafted to bring you to the precipice of the intellect over and over again so that when you see that you continually arrive at the same place, you may feel the only option left is to jump into the unknown and fall willingly into freedom.

Before we begin, prepare yourself for the enchanting dance of challenge and resistance. Like a spirited horse encountering an unfamiliar jump, you may initially pause, captivated by the obstacle before you. In that moment, a symphony of thoughts and emotions will unfold, echoing the natural inclination to preserve the comfort of what is known. But don't let your spirit waver, for with each graceful loop and determined stride, you can transcend the boundaries of your perceived limitations. Just as a majestic horse summons its inner bravery, so too can you summon the depths of your courage and embrace the uncharted realms of understanding. Feel the vibrant resonance of neural pathways weaving together, illuminating the way forward with each leap of faith. In this graceful pursuit, you will enjoy the profound beauty that lies in embracing new perspectives, and witness the harmonious symphony of your mind expanding and evolving.

Embrace the shimmering possibility that awaits, as you navigate the rhythmic currents of resistance and engage on a quest that transcends the boundaries of what you once held true. For within any transformative journey, the seeds of wisdom and enlightenment take root, blossoming into the exquisite flower of self-discovery.

You may wonder where this path leads, and question the value of forging new neural pathways based on the destination. Assessing the value of something through future projection is a valuable tool so allow me to share a quote that might inspire you to reconsider the obstacle and take another leap.

In 2021 Professor Brian Cox shed light on the understanding astrophysicists have gained about black holes, in the BBC series *Universe*. He succinctly summarised it as follows:

> *"Black holes are telling us that our intuitive picture of reality, of space and time, is wrong. The idea that this place is close to this place and that time ticks along, is wrong. There is a deeper picture of reality in which space and time, do not exist. Space and Time...are not fundamental properties of nature. They emerge from a deeper reality in which neither exist."*

This is precisely what I wish to show you and share with you, - the deeper reality from which Time itself emerges.

This book is composed of interconnected concepts that form a unified schema and while the format follows a chronological order, it's important to note that the concepts are interdependent and can be understood in various sequences.

Although there is no definitive 'first' concept, for the purpose of a coherent narrative, it will be presented as such, taking you on a journey through time and the exploration of these ideas.

Knowledge without potential application, holds limited value. To provide a starting point for practical application, I have included six chapters: Memory, Conditional Living, The Human Performance, God, Gravitation, and Evolution.

If you are ready, let's begin.

REBIRTH

I

BEING

When contemplating the nature of existence, a profound and perplexing question arises: "Why is there Something rather than Nothing?" Throughout history, various attempts have been made to tackle this question. One explanation suggests the existence of an "infinitesimally small point" with infinite properties, including gravity, density, and energy. This primordial point, existing "before time," underwent rapid expansion, giving birth to the Universe and unfolding the grand theatre of space, time, eggs, chickens, and all the rest of the drama and dance.

Many religions claim that God or a god was before all of this and created the universe through choice. Some mathematicians claim that mathematics existed prior to the Universe. Some believe information is the fundamental nature of reality and existed prior to all of this... somethingness.

When contemplating these various explanations for the existence of the universe, it becomes evident that all of these proposals revolve around different conceptions of 'something.' Whether it is a divine being, a mathematical structure, or an informational framework, these ideas all posit the existence of a fundamental entity or principle. None of these perspectives address the question from the standpoint of absolute nothingness. Instead, they offer different interpretations of the nature and origins of this 'somethingness.'

The proposed explanations for the origin of the universe, while fascinating, do not directly address the question of why there is something rather than nothing. Instead, they focus on elucidating how a particular event or entity could lead to the existence of the cosmos as we know it. However, these explanations all presuppose the existence of an initial event or entity that serves as the starting point for the cascade of events. Whether it is mathematics, information, an infinitesimally small point, or a chosen deity, they all assume the presence of something from which everything else unfolds. The question of why there is something rather than nothing remains unanswered by these explanations, as they still rely on a fundamental existence of 'something' to account for the existence of the universe.

Why isn't 'Nothing' prevailing over all existence? Let's look at the question directly. First, it's probably best to define the terms in the question so that we all know what we mean when we use them.

"Why is there Something rather than Nothing?"

| 1 | 2 | 3 | 4 |

1 - *Why is there...*

If I ask "why is there..." I feel like I'm requesting a reason for, or information about, some situation that is. Perhaps it's a request for a purpose or, a form of comparison.

I could ask of someone with an apple on their head, "Why is there an apple on your head?" I'm looking for a reason, a rationale, regarding the situation of an apple being on your head. It's odd. This often leads us to look to the past for an answer. 'I have an apple on my head because you asked me to, so that you could make a point.'

If the question were phrased as: 'What is the purpose of the apple being on your head?' purpose implies future. Purpose is then reason gained from the past, projected into the future: 'Why are there two loaves of bread in the cupboard?' 'So that we don't run out over the weekend.'

Posing the question at all also carries the implication that the situation may be unreasonable or abnormal by comparison to some other (perhaps 'more rational' or more commonplace) situation. For instance, "Why is there an apple on your head (as opposed to it being in a fruit bowl)?"

We'll take all three meanings into this investigation:
  · Reason based on the past
  · Purpose based on a potential future outcome, and
  · Comparison to a different circumstance that could be the case instead.

2 - *Something*

In the context of the question being asked, the word 'Something' is used to represent reality as we know it; existence itself in its entirety without omission; the actuality and totality of existence; the blatant and undeniable truth that being is.

'Something' is then used as a synonym for 'existence'. It doesn't seem like any other definition of 'Something' would allow us to fully answer the question.

3 - ... *rather than...*

The phrase 'rather than' is comparative. It follows on from 'why is there...' going on to suggest a different scenario and so setting up one concept against another. In answering a question posed like this, we're looking to understand more about both concepts. We look to understand their relationship to each other and their individual relationship to the situation. 'Why is there a carrot in my hand and not a chocolate bar?' 'Because you're trying to be healthier and a carrot is healthier for you than chocolate.'

In the context of our original question, this phrase is used to define 'something' and 'nothing' as inherently different and separate realities - supposing it is possible for them to be compared.

So far, the terms are defined so that we can ask the question a little more explicitly. The question is a request for a reason, and/or a purpose, and/or a comparison, regarding the fact of existence being the case as opposed to 'nothing'. What then, is this 'nothing'?

4 - *Nothing*

I don't feel there is any value in comparing this something that we know, observe and experience, with a theoretical one that we do not know, observe or experience. I'm also not looking for a relative 'nothing' as in, "There is nothing in the fridge".

By using 'nothing' in the context of this question, what we really want to compare to something is a total *absence* of all something-ness. Based on the definition of something, nothing therefore means absence of existence. It means *non-existence, non-being*.

Feel free to take a few moments to contemplate complete absence. Is it possible?

What is your experience of nothing?

The full question is now more transparent. It is a request for a reason and/or purpose and/or comparison, regarding the observable fact that existence is the case, and non-existence is NOT the case.

We're asking why non-existence doesn't exist, and why existence exists.

If you let that question sit with you now, reason, purpose or comparison, what comes back?

When seeking a reason from the past, it becomes clear that existence *is* because non-existence cannot have existed in the past. Thus, the continuity of existence is undeniable: existence is all there has ever been.

If we're asking for a purpose for the future, the answer is also clear. Non-existence will *never* exist in the future, therefore existence will always be.

If we look at the present we see that right now, non-existence isn't, and existence is.

If we're asking for a comparison to understand the relationship between them, perhaps we must go a little deeper.

If non-existence were to exist, what form would it take? Wouldn't it become a 'something' that exists? It seems that any manifestation of 'non-existence' would inherently be a form of existence. So is a state of non-existence possible? And if so, what would that state be like?

A state of non-existence would necessarily have to be devoid of any and all *existent* properties. This means there'd be no things, no matter present whatsoever.

The space that would contain those things also can't be present. This state also couldn't 'be' or exist for any length of time either. It would therefore be completely timeless and spaceless. This 'state of non-existence' would be o energy in o volume space for o amount of time. This state would necessarily never end because actually, having never existed in or as time, never even began in the first place.

Is a state that never was, is or will be, a state? It's a description of an environment of no environment. A state of non-existence is inherently paradoxical and self-defeating, defying the very notion of statehood.

Whatever it is we might think about when trying to imagine 'nothingness' with the mind, *cannot* be it. Nothingness does not exist as an objective reality because then it is a something. It also cannot be a subjective reality because then it is a perspective. This necessarily means that total non-existence - Nothingness - is endlessly, beginninglessly and infinitely non-existent. Forever.

Proposing even the *possibility* of non-existence somehow existing prior to (or instead of) existence is in fact, totally meaningless.

The implications for 'existence' are even more profound. Since complete non-existence is inherently impossible, it logically follows that existence must be eternal and infinite. Moreover, this eternal existence is not some distant concept, it is unfolding right now in this present moment.

Take a moment to truly contemplate this. See, right now, that *you* are existing. You are present! Whatever it is that you are, you exist, and so you *are necessarily* that *same* eternity of being.

To propose that you are not that which is, is to propose that you do not exist. From where could you possibly declare this? - Only from existence. You are that. You even say it yourself: "I am."

As yet, we don't really know what existence is made of; the nature of its activity or the extent of itself. So, if you're ready to continue, let's keep going.

*

Is it the case that 'something' held in this hand, and 'nothing' not held at all, are really opposites of one another? Can we genuinely compare them?

On one hand, non-existence is inherently characterised by its absence, by its sheer lack of presence. Paradoxically, does this absence imply that non-existence, by not being, manifests as a form of being - present as absence itself?

It's a strange one.

The only way to grasp the concept of non-existence would be through reflection on its absence. Standing in front of a mirror you say, "Here I am, caught in the act of being! Non-existence, the sly trickster, can only be noticed when it's nowhere to be found!"

So again, does the *absence* of nothingness only help to demonstrate its existence? Every moment that existence is, non-existence is NOT. Are the two happening simultaneously?

Take a few moments to contemplate this paradox. Observe your surroundings. Everything that you perceive through your senses, conceive within your mind, and become aware of, including your very awareness itself, is intricately intertwined with the absence of non-existence. It is within this absence that the essence of all things unfolds: a profound presence. Consider the sheer magnitude of this realisation. In every breath you take, in every experience you encounter, you *are* the eternal present.

Existence and non-existence cannot be truly considered as relative or separate from one another. As we delve deeper into their essence, we begin to perceive their inherent interconnection and the seamless continuum they comprise.

The notions of 'something' and 'nothing,' or existence and non-existence, appear to dissolve into an indivisible reality.

Consider this: Existence does not strive to overcome or move towards total oblivion, for it already *is* total oblivion. It is akin to a state of perfect balance, a sublime harmony. However, the term 'balance' typically implies the reconciliation of opposing forces, whereas in this context, no such opposition is evident.

Instead, we find ourselves immersed in a profound unity, where existence and non-existence converge into an ineffable whole. It is within this enigmatic realm that the true nature of reality unveils itself, transcending the boundaries of dualistic concepts.

So where does the supposed opposition between existence and non-existence arises from? It seems to me to be out of the fabrication of a *concept* of non-existence as an existing void. This setup creates an illusion of division where, upon thorough investigation, there really doesn't seem to be any.

If this perceived division is taken as fundamental it could, I imagine, lead to further perceived divisions off the back of it. This fundamental split between existing and not existing would lead to such supposed states as alive and dead, awake and asleep, self and other, and so to innumerable concepts in a finite, dualistic reality. However, any culture that rides the wave of finitude, bound by its inherent limitations, will eventually find itself dissolving on the shores of its own transience. The nature of the finite is such that it cannot endure indefinitely.

Given that there is no inherent division between existence and non-existence, as it's primarily a conceptual distinction, these two terms shouldn't truly exist as separate entities. Beyond their individual conceptual frameworks i.e. in reality, they are synonymous. In an attempt to capture this unified essence, I'd like to consolidate them into a single word.

Drawing inspiration from the practice of combining different terms into a single character, as seen in Japanese or Chinese writing, we find a good example in the term 'Advaita' used in ancient Eastern traditions.[1] While this term aligns with the idea, it carries with it a complex web of associated traditions and interpretations, so we will avoid this for now to avoid confusion.

Therefore, I have chosen the term 'Being' as a concise expression of this unification. It encapsulates the essence of both existence and non-existence without the need for a conceptual divide. By utilising this single word, we aim to convey the underlying unity that transcends the limitations of dualistic thinking and can use it in subsequent chapters as we move forward.

I chose 'Being' because it is not a statement about something else, it is self-contained and self-describing. Being is what is, is neither a noun that could lend itself to a particular image, nor a verb that is carried out by something specific. It is somewhere in between noun and verb. Being is also non-exclusive. It is common to everything that could be known, experienced, imagined, or lived. Being is absolutely equal in every sense as there isn't anything that could be seen as less than or unworthy of Being, because, by virtue of being known, is already Being itself.

*

There are a few things that may seem to have been blown past and not really investigated; concepts like eternity, infinity and

---

[1] Literally translated: '*a*' = non-, 'dvaita' = dual.

finitude; or like the nature of the *activity* of Being, such as rocks and trees and humans and fire and physics and so on.

We're going to investigate these now, starting with the profound realms of Infinity, Eternity and Finitude.

2

Infinity

Is Infinity a concept? It's a common belief that it is, but a concept is only an idea. Is infinity an idea? There is a thought experiment called *The Infinite Hotel,* and it is ordinarily used to demonstrate the vastness of infinity. It goes like this:

> *The Infinite Hotel has infinitely many rooms and they're all occupied. Nevertheless, if you arrive without a booking, the kind staff working there will be able to find a room for you to sleep in. They can do this because they can move the guest in room one to room two, and the guest in room two to room three and so on. There are 'infinitely many' rooms, and so they can always make space for one more guest.*

This suggests that infinity can be seen as an unending quantity of finite elements, exemplified by the countless rooms in the hotel. It portrays infinity as an abstract pattern, a mathematical concept born from the interplay of finite entities. Indeed, some mathematical formulas have been created to demonstrate different 'types' of infinity. The logical inference here is that this comes from a perspective that believes finitude is the foundation of reality; that infinity is *made of* finitude.

Viewing it like this, mathematics becomes somewhat deified, believed to deal in counting, multiplying, dividing and subtracting actualities. It positions human understanding as the arbiter of reality. It's an interesting position to take, but, by acknowledging the intrinsic limitations of this viewpoint, we open ourselves to broader possibilities beyond the confines of finitude, inviting a more expansive exploration of the nature of existence.

It may be the case that the purpose of *The Infinite Hotel* is not to establish the primacy of finitude. Rather, it could be an endeavour to provide a glimpse of infinity by presenting it in terms of familiar concepts and finite structures. However, it is precisely in this attempt to confine infinity within the boundaries of our understanding that we fall flat on our face.

Let's look at it again, this time bringing in the understanding of Being. After all, if this knowledge can't be applied to our experience, what good is it?

Imagine you are sitting in a field, or, sit in a field. Look outward. Extend your imagination outward, envisioning the environment stretching infinitely in all directions.

Do you see this infinity all at once, an entire never-ending-ness and totally without limit? Or, is it effectively a continuous succession of single and limited thoughts? Are your thoughts centred on what lies beyond the next horizon: another planet, galaxy, or star, more space?

These thoughts, though captivating, are finite in nature. They are conceptual objects, existing within the realm of our mental constructs. Distances, timescales, colossal and minuscule objects - they are all finite elements within the image our minds can conjure.

In essence, our conceptualisation is rooted in finitude, and we're only *implying* that it goes on forever by projecting our finite notions into the distant future.

We aren't conceptualising forever-ness of infinity. There are no infinite thoughts present because that is simply not the nature of thought. Thought is, as you just observed, the use and manipulation of finite images.

How *could* you have an infinite thought? It couldn't be thought about it because it can't be defined in terms of finitude. It's not that the edge would be so big we can't imagine it, it's that it wouldn't have such thing as an edge to be imagined.

Finitude is measure, differentiation, boundary and limitation. On the other hand, infinity, by its very essence as 'non-finite,' cannot be fundamentally bound by finitude. While it may contain elements of finitude within it, its fundamental nature transcends the limitations of finitude. Infinity must therefore be measureless, undifferentiated, without boundary and completely limitless in every way. No beginning, no end, no middle.

Now, is this a concept?

When we attempt to use our imagination to conceive of a measureless and limitless infinity, we find that our mental constructs inherently involve boundaries, measurements, and comparisons. Any concept we create, by its very nature, has some form of limitation as it defines and distinguishes some things from others. Infinity, however, defies such limitations. It can't be adequately defined or contained within *any* conceptual frameworks without contradicting its inherent nature. A truly limitless and measureless, undifferentiated and shape-less, boundary-less and timeless *object* is an oxymoron.

An object is an object because it has 'values' in the world of comparison and measure. Values like height, width, roughness, sweetness, rate of vibration and so on. Consequently no individual o*bject (mental or physical)* can be infinite. Therefore, infinity is not an object or a particular *property* of an object. This means infinity can't be in any sense conceptual. Infinity is beyond the scope of conceptualisation.

Only finite 'things' like numbers, oranges, chairs and personas can be conceptual. So in fact is it the reverse? Is it that finitude is conceptual? Is finitude *entirely* conceptual?

If we consider that every finite object or concept is an abstraction from the infinite, it implies that the reality of these finite entities is dependent on and derived from the infinite reality of Being. This would mean no finite thing has any independent reality of its own. It could never exist *outside* of Being, in other words. All of its reality would be *given to it* by the infinite reality from which the finite ideas and objects were abstracted.

I wonder, where did we get the definition of a second? Didn't we just, make it up? Like meters. There are no 'seconds' as independent realities, only our concept of 'a second' exists. "It's about... that long." It's the same with a meter: "It's about... that long," said some human with arms out wide.

But, other humans came along and didn't really like these definitions being so loose, so they decided to define the second based on a particular observation, something perceived to be stable, regular, and consistent - just like the idea of a second. We eventually end up with atomic clocks, whereby a second is defined by a particular number of vibrations made by a particular atom.[2]

The observation is the vibrating, and from it emerges the abstraction of 'a second.' This abstraction is then employed to 'measure' the reality from which it originated: "A caesium atom oscillates 9,192,631,770 times every second." Consider the shift that occurs here – now its inside out. The initial abstraction is not an independent reality but rather a reference point for all other abstractions. If we attempt to comprehend reality solely through finite abstractions, we inevitably find ourselves in a relativistic state, one that is fundamentally dualistic and fragmented.

We can forget where the abstraction came from and come to believe that, because it accords with observation so well, it represents the true nature of reality. Observe this closely. Abstraction, to be useful at all, must be projected back onto its source. Yet, to assume that the source itself is composed of what has been abstracted from it is an error.

What is abstracted is entirely contingent upon the perspective through which we perceive reality. Other living beings on this planet, and quite possibly on other planets as well, will engage in different modes of abstraction or comprehension based on their unique perceptual capacities. It is important to recognise here that perceptions are inherently limitations.

In the pursuit of understanding and counting, it is possible that humanity is not uncovering some ultimate objective reality, but rather gaining insight into its own mode

---

[2] 9,192,631,770 oscillations of a caesium atom is a definition of 'one second'.

of perception. Naturally this raises the question: What is perceiving?

Again we say, "I am".

So is consciousness, awareness, an object that is perceived or is it that which is perceiving?

If consciousness were an object to be perceived, it would necessarily possess limitations. Try the scientific approach with this. In your own experience of consciousness, can you discern any boundaries, edges, or objective qualities? Is there any aspect of consciousness that can be clearly defined as a separate entity?

Should you discover an objective quality or object within consciousness, the inquiry deepens: Are you that object or quality, or are you that which is aware of it?

Are you identified with what you are conscious of, or are you, in fact, consciousness itself?

*

Infinity is not finite; not abstraction; not concept. It doesn't make sense to shackle infinity to a concept of individuality anymore than to chain it to the abstract mathematical concept of continuous counting - the 'never-ending' series. By confining infinity to the pattern of continuous finite concepts (numerical or otherwise), we also bind it to the concept of time, of sequence. It is then also tethered to being the *result* of some operation between two or more finite objects: a sum - albeit a continuously repeating one - and this immediately seems to me, to be a very grave error.

The fallacy of attempting to construct infinity through the combination of finite objects is haunting both the realm of physics and spiritual exploration. Whether it's the physicist seeking unity among particles or the spiritual seeker seeking unity among psychological phenomena, the underlying question remains the same. Can two finite objects create or *construct* infinity?

As we already know, the answer is no. No matter how large or diverse the numbers or events we combine, the result will always be finite in nature. Any finite number added to another finite number yields, you guessed it, a finite number. Similarly, any event arising from two causes is inherently finite because it has a beginning.

I put it to you that the uncountable nature of infinity does not stem from the sheer quantity of things to measure. Rather, it lies in the fact that infinity exists outside the realm of counting and measurement altogether. Infinity transcends the limitations of finite concepts, defying our attempts to confine it within the framework of counting and measuring.

Pi does not have "infinitely many" digits; infinity is not a *quantity*. Quantity is measure, and measure is finite. The never-ending series, be it Pi or *The Infinite Hotel,* is not an 'infinite' series but simply a continuous one consisting of adding conceptual finite intervals to previous conceptual finite values.

Pi, and other irrational numbers like it, are perhaps better framed as finitude's attempt at conceptualising, imagining, or displaying infinity in mathematical / conceptual terms.

Pi is what happens when there is an attempt to measure infinity. The infinity of the circle is in its loop. It doesn't seem to 'progress' from A to B like a line does. It is self-contained and has no orientation or direction. The circle's circumference - its immediacy - is divided into smaller and smaller fragments by simply splitting the previous measure-concept into two smaller concepts of measure.

The process of determining Pi mirrors the workings of the mind itself. Spontaneous finite measure is eternally generate-able because the *context* from and in which finitude appears is absolutely limitless. Again, looking for the context of thought, do you find limit?

So it's clear. Infinity isn't any particular object or concept, nor is it the further abstraction of the counting or 'measuring' of those objects or concepts; it is without limit in every way. It can't be limited to or by time, space, thought, concept or duality of any kind. Due to this, the profound realisation may unfold itself: that infinity must therefore mean *everything, everywhere, at all times simultaneously.*

It can't even be limited to 'not being finite,' which means all finite appearances can only be, fundamentally, forms or 'manifestations' if you like, of the underlying infinity of Being.

What you are looking *at* AND where you are looking *from*, right now, is infinity.

We can divide it any way we please: into thirds, into objects and subjects, into causes and effects, into kittens and not-kittens, into people and environments. There cannot be any *actual* division.

If reality exists divided and isolated, made up of finite independently existing tiny parts or, 'particles', we are inevitably brought back to the question of 'Why is there something rather than nothing?' From this view there must have been a beginning to what is finite, and so seek an explanation why all this finitude began at all, and around and around we go.

Upon closer examination, it becomes evident that viewing reality as a unified whole is a more reasonable approach. If we try to run away from this conclusion, the only purpose that seems to serve is to preserve a belief in finitude, which, if we think about it, is inherently limited. We only limit our thinking, our understanding and our potential... What for?

When we do that, we have to perpetually conceive of bigger or more elaborate finite systems of energy like a multiverse because it's the only way to explain anything in a finite system: by dependence upon something other than itself.[3] Nothing is allowed to be self-existent because every finite *thing, must* have a cause preceding it: an explanation in time.

*

By dissolving the misconception of countable or constructed infinities, we can also transcend the limitations imposed upon the concept of eternity and recognise its inherent connection to the boundless expanse of infinity.

The recognition of infinity as the substrate of all finitude makes the mathematical notion of different 'types' of infinity redundant. Infinity is everything all at once; there can't really be 'types' of *everything*. What would be an alternate way for 'everything simultaneously' to be the case? I can't see it at least. The 'types of infinity' are simply types or ways in which we could begin and then continue to count endlessly; but again, this is a process finite in nature; it's temporal.

Infinity, by its very nature, transcends the confines of time. It exists in a state of timelessness while encompassing all moments. Eternity, therefore, is not an endless continuation but rather the perpetual presence of infinity. As for the concept of the big bang, it can be seen as a moment of immense creation within the cosmic unfolding, without necessitating the beginning of Being itself. The issue arises only if we attribute the big bang as the starting point of infinity, which would now contradict logical understanding.

The latter belief - that of a beginning to Being - seems only to be based on a traditional narrative of beginnings

---

[3] External dependency as an explanatory method is worth taking note of at this point.

gleaned solely from the observation of time. A tale told from the point of view of a finite perspective.

A beginning is a cause and effect notion, and causation is time and, time is finite. If we decide to say, as Aristotle did, the beginning is the uncaused cause, then *that* cause necessarily always was and so is no longer temporal.

The notion of an uncaused cause, as Aristotle proposed, suggests a timeless and eternal background from which all temporal events arise. This eternal background is infinity itself, encompassing the beginning and ending of all things. The apparent finitude of objects and time is merely an illusion arising from our limited perception within the unlimited eternity of omnipresent Being.

All of what we're discovering here is completely falsifiable. All we've done so far is look at what is, and then phrase it in terms of logic and make deductions based on observation. That's what the scientific method is based on. To prove this wrong, all one need do is investigate it for themselves and find it to be inconsistent with experience. This *is* actual experience we're exploring, not a hypothetical reality. We can even check this against scientific discoveries.

The field of physics has produced a model of reality that declares everything is made of tiny bits of some stuff they're not quite sure what it is just yet, and few people have a problem with that due to the adherence to the method of observation and deduction. Nevertheless, it is said that everything is made of atoms. Atoms are forms of mass, and mass is energy. Atoms then, are a pattern of energy. Thus the human organism is a pattern of patterns of energy. But given that every thing is made of energy, the only difference between a human and everything else is down to the particular shape the energy takes amid a cosmic ocean of only energy. In other words, if you were truly separate and not continuous with everything else, you wouldn't be here.

The main difference between the physical or materialist point of view and the one we've come to so far in this book however, is that we didn't begin the inquiry by arbitrarily assuming the conclusion that finitude is the foundation of reality.

It is of course apparent that matter seems to exist in some way. It is, for all intents and purposes, 'real'. We interact with it, we're grounded by it, we can throw it around, hug it, consume it... so what is it?

With a fervent spirit of inquiry, we turn our gaze towards the enigmatic force that shapes matter's dance: Time. Like a celestial conductor, time orchestrates the movements and transformations of matter, imbuing each moment with a sense of fleeting grace. Let's continue this profound investigation, as we delve into the depths of matter and unravel the mysteries that lie within the ever-unfolding majesty of time.

3

Process

What is time? 'Past, present, future' as a perceived *direction* of time is a very common way to think about it, but this is ostensibly a movement *of* time, not what time is. Nonetheless, this perspective can guide us in refining the question.

What, if it were removed from experience, would stop the perception of the movement from past to present to future? Take a couple of seconds to think about it.

It seems to me, that the only way we can tell the difference between a past event and a present or future event is through the observation of change. If we removed change from experience, the observation of time would be impossible.

If there is no change, necessarily there is no motion. Can you imagine something that never moves, yet changes? Rocks don't seem to move, but, looking more closely, we see movement of atoms, vibrations.

If change cannot happen without motion, it is logical to conclude that if there is no motion, there is no time. It is impossible to speak about movement, change or time as if independent of each other. They're one observation, needlessly divided into separate concepts.

Through observation we can see that everything is in motion and everything is changing. Everything is in process. So what are these *things* that are changing?

If we could somehow *remove* change, remove time, from any alleged concrete *thing* or *object*, what would happen to it? Wouldn't it just entirely cease to be what it was? For instance, what would remain of 'The Sun' if we stripped it of its processes?

Is there some platonic form of The Sun differentiated from its action? Is it like this?

The Shine →   The Sun

Would there be a *thing* that we would call The Sun? - A thing that doesn't shine or change or process in time? No, right? 'The Sun' is a linguistic abstraction; it's not something that exists truly independent from the *processes* of nuclear fusion, of heat, of electromagnetism and so on.

So it's not that The Sun exists prior and then *acts out* the processes of nuclear fusion, electromagnetism, etc., as some kind of agent. The Sun *is* its processes. The name 'The Sun' is like 'rain' or 'breath'. They're nouns created by the mind, from what is pure verb.

'The rain' is the process of water falling to Earth (raining), but there is no independent object 'rain'. 'The breath' is the process of inhalation and exhalation (breathing), but there is no independent object called 'breath'. Nouns are just labels we give to stable or common processes. Nature as perceived by the human organism - determined by the human senses - appears divided into objects, amidst the incontrovertible truth of entirely continuous process.

The same must be true of *any and every* noun that can be thought of, both abstract and 'concrete'. Any noun you can think of is a not actually a separate *thing* that is independent of the processes associated with it. If we stripped 'a plant' of all its process, what's left? We could say, 'a dead plant', but not really, because part of the process of 'plant' is to die and decay. The plant would simply vanish and leave nothing behind. You stopped the process, which means the atoms don't vibrate. If an atom doesn't vibrate then it has, or better, *is,* no energy. If there is no energy to an atom, there's nothing left of it, and so it isn't there. Atoms are not *made of* energy, they *are* energy, and energy is process. No process, no energy, no atoms, no plant.

Such is the essence of 'human' as well. The common sense is to say that the human is an agent and *does* the actions living, thinking, breathing, and so on. But again, without the processes there is no human left to talk about. So the processes of living, thinking, breathing, digesting etc. are inseparable from the overall on-going process: 'human'. The essence of being human resides not in static forms, but in the graceful flux of perpetual becoming.

The vibration of life appears to be layers of processes, like harmonics, all coming together to create a beautiful ensemble, perceived by the human process as 'objects'. The human process is constantly communicating and exchanging with what is believed to be 'outside' of it. Yet 'human process' does not exist if there is no air to continue breathing, and so actually the air that is being breathed is part of the same process 'human'.

So I ask you now, does process human exist in a separate environment?

We could say yes. The environment is separate from 'me' and I interact with it, which is outside me. Great. Now, if I am separate from it, and interact with it, it's strange to see that I can't choose *not* to interact with it. Like with the air pressure I'm living in to maintain the structure of my cells, or the oxygen and carbon-dioxide I'm breathing, or water I'm drinking, and so on. I totally depend upon it if I'm separate from it. And another mystery arises. If I *am* separate, where did I come from if not this environment? My parents? But they *are* part of my environment so I must conclude that I came *out of* the environment. So if I'm separate, then my parents must have come from somewhere else too?

When we prioritise observation over preconceived beliefs, a new perspective emerges. Instead of viewing the human process as separate from the environment, we recognise that it is intricately intertwined with and inseparable from it. Each action attributed to the human process - breathing, digesting, thinking - relies on the elements and processes of the environment. Rather than perceiving these actions as distinctively human, we can reframe them as manifestations of the larger environmental process, expressed through the subjective form we identify as 'human'. This shift in perception lays waste to the notion of separation and invites a deeper understanding of the interconnectivity between all supposed 'things' and the vast unfolding process of the entire cosmos.

Indeed, the interconnectedness of processes extends far beyond the realm of human existence. From galaxies to solar systems, from Earth to the tiniest organisms, from atomic particles to the complex workings of thought and speech, all are expressions of the totality in process. Each entity, regardless of its form or scale, emerges within and as an integral part of the ever-unfolding environment. There is a profound unity in the understanding that everything is a manifestation of the same continuous process, interconnected and interdependent in the grand symphony of existence.

The arbitrary distinctions we make based on sensory perceptions, such as size and scale, do not signify an end to the overall process. The seamless and continuous nature of the process transcends these divisions. Just as Dr. Sabine Hossenfelder eloquently expressed in her insights on Quantum Mechanics, even seemingly fundamental particles like quarks are not separate entities but rather mathematical models representing specific energy processes. If we extend this perspective to language as a whole, recognising that nouns are merely linguistic representations of sensory models of processes, a deeper coherence and unity in our understanding emerges. It opens up new possibilities for comprehending the interconnectedness and harmony that pervades the fabric of existence. And yet, this is merely the beginning, as there is much more to explore and uncover on this profound journey of understanding.

*

The named boundaries of the physical world - and language in general - are arbitrary. They are solely dependent upon how we choose to measure process. The intriguing nature of quantum mechanics exemplifies this, as the behaviour of an electron can appear as both a wave and a particle depending on how it is observed. Our perceptions and measurings of life, in a similar vein, shape our individual realities.

Our biggest mistake has been to attribute independent agency of action to each perceived boundary. We say: "Atoms vibrate," "stars shine," and "matter curves spacetime".

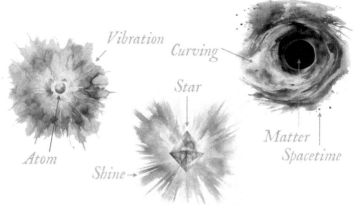

Observation shows clearly that life is not this way! Vibration *is* the atom, the shining *is* the star, and, THE CURVING OF SPACETIME *is* MATTER.

Process is change, is movement, is time.

Although it seems like the field of physics is studying solid things called particles or indeed 'strings', in reality it is only studying the movement of change, and thus exclusively studying time itself. There are no *things* as entities in their own right that *do an action* called *changing*. Such an object has never been found. Every apparent object has been shown to be simply what a particular group of smaller processes looks like from a distance.

There are no objects as fundamental realities; there is simply the miraculous changing.

With continued scale, process human for example, cannot see process atom except in enormous clusters. These clusters of processes make complexity, *unique* complexity, as no two whirlpools of collective process could be exactly the same.

In the conventional approach to investigation, we often explain the discoveries of these processes by translating them into relationships between objects. Naturally then we seek to understand what these objects are made of, and as we delve deeper, again we find that the answer leads us back to processes. However, in our attempt to satisfy the mind's inclination towards objects, we then reframe the explanation in terms of objects in relationship. It becomes a continuous cycle of translating processes into objects, and objects into processes.

When we figure reality this way, motion and time are seen as intellectual measurements of the assumed fundamental reality: the finite objects. Again, here is the belief that reality is actually divided and finite. Within this framework, all measurements become abstract and arbitrary systems that rely on observing relative movement, specifically movement in relation to an external frame of reference.

The ordinary view of time depicts it as a measurement of object relationships, relative and abstract. Yet, objects are not actualities but pockets of stable process. Thus, time becomes an abstract measurement of relationships between abstractions - a mere reflection, veiling the essence of time itself.

Using the ordinary view of time, if we want to know more about an object we must split it into smaller objects in order to provide the relativistic conditions that allow us to use the method of calculation we understand in order to describe it. Humans that take this line of investigation therefore understand the world only in terms of the method of calculation they're using. While the method may appear to match reality, scientific investigations repeatedly demonstrate that the notion of distinct 'objects' separate from process lacks evidence.

It is the way in which humans view the world that provides both the measurement system and the result. The result is invariably used to back up the validity of the measurement system used to achieve it, perpetuating a feedback loop of cognitive bias.

The idea that there must be some 'thing' to change in order for there to be a process of change seems intuitive. But what we perceive as a 'thing' is actually an emergent result born from pure changing process. It is instead clear that the changing or the process is fundamental, not the object.

The concept of separate and distinct objects, with solid boundaries and fixed properties, seems to be a product of our perceptual limitations, rather than an accurate representation of the true nature of reality. It is not only possible, but almost certain that common understanding of the world among humanity is influenced by the particular nature of the human organism, and that there is a more expansive and interconnected reality beyond the beautiful (though limited) perspective we are afforded with the senses.

Some humans search for the ultimate foundation, hoping to prove that process emerges from finite objects, the 'building blocks' of reality. They ponder concepts like vibrating strings in multiple dimensions. Yet, even in these theories, we encounter the essential element of process—the very word 'vibrating.' It seems that time, with its indispensable role, persists as the key to understanding everything and anything.

The ordinary view of time as a pervasive entropy-line from past to future, enacting decay upon innocent matter, involves the insertion of a ghost into physics - an external agency that manipulates the world of form. It is the insertion of a god: the god of death manipulating the world of life.

But let us dare to spin the prism of perception and invert the paradigm entirely. What if we release the notion of time as a mere abstract dimension influencing objectivity, and instead embrace it as the very foundation of objective reality? How would we conceive of time when matter is inseparable from it?

4

THREE-DIMENSIONAL TIME

Up to this point our investigation has shown that existence is eternal and infinite but nevertheless there are undoubtedly finite forms - finite appearances - that can be perceived.

These finite appearances must always be processes. They are motion, they are *all* energy and energy *is* vibration. Depending on the pattern of the vibration, the form is different. If we look at multiple different patterns vibrating together, we have the beginnings of complexity. When an orchestra play together the music is more complex than if just one instrument vibrates on its own.

Bees are themselves a pattern of vibration. Vibration pattern 'bee' does so in harmony with the vibration pattern 'flower'. This is often called symbiosis, that of two independent organisms living together; but in this new model, symbiosis is simply a complex pattern of vibration, like music: the bee-flower harmony. The appearance of them being separate is like looking at two sides of a coin. Although they *appear* separate, they can't actually be separated, and if they are, the entire system breaks down. If you remove the strings from a violin body, you can't get music out of either piece.

Let's delve deeper into the nature of vibration. Conventionally, we envision vibration as a two-dimensional wave, a representation of the movement of particles or the generation of energy unfolding over or 'through' time. Like this:

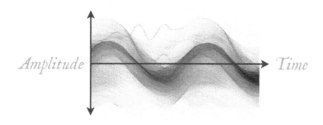

However, this perspective implies a separation between vibration and time, as if they exist independently, as if an entity called "energy" *moves* through a separate field called 'time'. But let's pause and reflect. Can we truly conceive of vibration devoid of time? Likewise, how could we even contemplate the concept of time without the underlying essence of vibration, of movement? Vibration is movement, is process, and is perhaps the very essence of time itself.

Could a finite object or entity possibly *enact* TIME? In order to do this the object or entity would need to preexist itself to create the environment for its own existence, and then emerge into being, so that it can then create itself as an object in time...

This is silly.

In clinging to the notion of a finite-object reality, we come to a critical juncture: we're either going to have to begin postulating finite objects outside of time, that is, infinite finites - running ourselves into an intellectual cul-de-sac; or liberate ourselves from preconceptions and embrace a profound shift in perspective.

Vibration transcends being a mere *function* of entities in time; rather, entities themselves emerge as expressions of Time itself. Put more directly, objects *are Time*.

What I imagine would stop us from accepting this, is the idea that vibration is an activity *of* something. We give the vibration a beginning point, an end point and a measurement in between.[4] We see movement, infer object and then say it is the object that moves.

See Movement   *Infer Object*   *Invert it*

*

The type of vibration characterised by polarity, opposition, and duality is a limited representation and fails to capture the richness of observation.

What then, is the vibration of reality in three dimensions?

We understand that everything is fundamentally vibration, from atoms at the microscopic scale to stars, planets, and galaxies at the cosmic scale. However, the linear, two-dimensional motion depicted in the graph seems inadequate when considering the principles of inertia in the vast expanse of space. It would defy numerous laws of physics to suggest that an object vibrates by abruptly changing direction in a seemingly random manner, oscillating back and forth without any

---

[4] The psychological projection of a human life perhaps?

discernible pattern or cause.

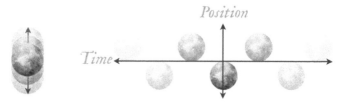

In astrophysics if there were sight of a star doing this, the search would be on for something else that was causing this bizarre movement. This idea is not vibration in three dimensions, it is a two dimensional *representation* of vibration, superimposed into three dimensions, which fails to provide a comprehensive understanding. So, what is vibration in three dimensions?

Consider this: everything in the universe, regardless of scale, fundamentally arises from the same process of vibration or energy. So if we can identify the most prevalent process that resonates throughout the cosmos we will likely come across the answer. The most prevalent process is, of course, spin.

If everything is vibration, everything is spin in some form or another. They're the same! But it isn't a spin *of* anything, it's the spin itself, the vortex, the suction and repulsion that whips up the mirage of a static object that is spinning. Picture a swirling vortex in a river, we call it 'a whirlpool,' but the whirlpool has no independent reality that means it could be removed from the water and maintained in your hands. It's an inseparable part of the flowing water, a beautiful pattern that emerges within it. The appearances of objects - atoms, planets, even us - are just like these whirlpools: intricate formations of universal vibration, but never separate entities in isolation.

This would mean that the 'object' never moves *through* time as a separate entity in an environment, because in fact, as an illusion of spin itself, the object is entirely *made of* Time.

Objects, and so mass, and so energy, is Time.

Time is a mesmerising manifestation of infinite Being, crafting the illusion of finitude through its dance. Time is not an elusive intangible; it is right here in front of us! Every object is a captivating spectacle, a symphony of Time's expression, a composition of its essence. Each entity is a dynamic performance, an exquisite formulation, an embodiment of Time - a living *Time-form.*

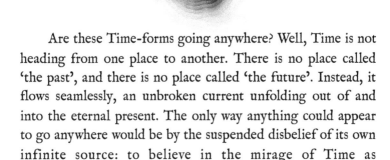

Are these Time-forms going anywhere? Well, Time is not heading from one place to another. There is no place called 'the past', and there is no place called 'the future'. Instead, it flows seamlessly, an unbroken current unfolding out of and into the eternal present. The only way anything could appear to go anywhere would be by the suspended disbelief of its own infinite source: to believe in the mirage of Time as fundamental.

Magnetic fields show a pattern of timeless unfolding. No beginning, no end, just huge loops of energy radiation and absorption as the same moment.

It's strange that our clocks are cyclical yet our idea of time is different. We *know* time is cycles, layers of cycles, cycles of cycles! The seasons cycle, we talk about the life cycle of plants and stars, orbits are cycles. Time isn't triumphantly marching objects to a place called 'future.' Time is born of eternity, floods into the present, and shimmers back into eternity. Like the 24-hour cycle, it comes, endures, and dissolves back into itself. If Time marches anywhere, it is around in a circle, spinning itself: the graceful dance of eternal freedom, a spontaneous self-radiation of Time, the unfolding of eternity into itself.

As eternity is not any particular *thing* it will never stick in one shape. It will always be changing and therefore it is, paradoxically, unchanging in this regard.

What we see as objects, as Time-forms, are perceptions of boundaries, limits of stability of certain processes, entirely based on the senses of the perceiver.

Based on the nature of the perception, Time-boundaries can be considered relative to the scale of the perceiver. It may be a giant sphere of hydrogen and helium appearing to burn with a blazing light for time unknowable. It may be a giant structure of fibres and bark with roots drinking from the depths of the Earth with leaves that convert that blazing light into sugars to grow and reach for the stars, attempting to bridge the gap between heaven and Earth. Time-boundaries may be invisible yet detectable with giant instruments the size of cities; or, it may be the human being that you feel you are right now. These are all perceptions of naught but Time.

Now, let's turn our attention to Thermodynamics, specifically to the concept of Entropy, which pervades our understanding of the physical world. Entropy tells us that energy tends to disperse and reach a state of equilibrium, gradually dissipating into uniformity. Considering that energy is synonymous with Time, it follows that Time itself radiates. Thus, everything we perceive is a manifestation of Time, radiating Time.

As Time radiates, what implications does this have for the surrounding environment? We can draw an analogy using heat. Imagine being outside on a cool night and lighting a fire. As the fire progresses through its initial stages, it settles into a steady state, emitting a consistent and comforting warmth. As you position yourself closer to the center of the fire, you feel a greater intensity of heat. Conversely, as you move away from the center, the temperature gradually decreases. You notice that the heat from the fire dissipates into a larger area as you move further away from its core. This creates a gradient of heat based on distance, and the entire field of heat is 'the fire.'

Bird's eye view

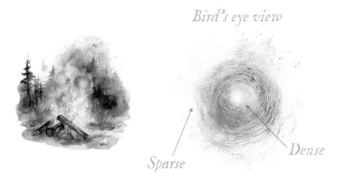

Sparse

Dense

Similarly, the radiating nature of Time creates a vast field of Time that permeates the environment. Just as the heat of the fire spreads outward, the influence of Time extends into the deepest reaches of the universe, shaping the perception and experiences within its resonance. We see a denser field of Time closer to the center, gradually transitioning into a sparser field as we move away. This elongated and stretched field of Time is a result of the dissipation of energy that was initially radiated.

In this revelation, a remarkable environment comes into focus - a 'Time-Gradient Environment.' Within this environment, a dense central spinning sphere-like boundary of radiating Time emerges, resembling the core of the fire. As we move further from the center, the influence of Time gradually diminishes, akin to the dissipation of heat as we move away from the fire.

In the scenario of the fire, we can detect the heat with our senses, contrasting it with the coldness of the surrounding night air. There is, seemingly, a separate environment into which the heat dissipates. Now let's inquire: is the same true for Time?

What would be the environment into which Time dissipates? Space? If we look out into the vast expanse of the universe with humanity's best telescopes, what do we see? Do we observe objects in space, or do we see pure unfolding process? It's in this distinction that the concept of a distinct environment, a space for objects to exist in, emerges. Without the notion of space defining their boundaries, objects cease to be objects, having no border to make them distinct from what they are not.

However, if we shift our perspective and see the unfolding of processes instead of discrete objects, there needn't be the postulate of a spatial dimension because there are no objects as realities unto themselves. Instead, we come to realise that there is only Time - a continuous flow of process. The so-called 'environment' can be easily understood as temporal, existing as a manifestation of Time itself, albeit in a less concentrated form.

In fact, when we investigate what we have conventionally been referring to as 'space,' we see that it's not some vast emptiness, but relentlessly teeming with quantum fluctuations. These fluctuations are energy process, which is still only Time, just on a scale so small that it boggles the human mind! These quantum fluctuations, often described as "virtual particles popping in and out of existence," can be reimagined as moments of Time's creation and destruction; universes appearing and timing-out on a scale so small that the human can't perceive them as individual experiences. They resemble transient wormholes, momentarily opening, releasing Time, and then closing again—an eternal dance of creation.

In light of this understanding, the concept of empty space loses its substance. There is no actual void anywhere. If we could *see* these quantum events, we'd never have imagined such a thing as 'space' existed at all. It's only because we don't or didn't see them that we postulated the existence of space. However, space, just like objects and the environment, does not possess an independent existence. It too, is part of the mirage; the boundaries of objects and space dissolve into the shimmering background of infinity.

We can instead begin to speak of distances of time, we can talk of movement through Time as movement through what we have been calling 'space'. In this perspective, the concept of a distinct 'time-environment' and a distinct 'time-form' are used merely to transition to this deeper point of view where there is only time. The terms become obsolete, for they are not separate processes. The unfolding of galaxies, stars, planets, plants, people, and the distances in between them are in fact the same underlying process of Time, manifesting itself at different distances and scales.

By embracing this perspective, we transcend the conventional dichotomy between time and space. We recognise that they are the same universal process. Just as galaxies whirl in cosmic dances and stars navigate their celestial paths, all physical manifestations *are* the continuous flow of Time. Whether on a grand cosmic scale or in the subtleties of our personal experiences, the underlying process remains unchanged.

Therefore, let us release the notion of separation and instead perceive the magnificent unity of the cosmos. It is a seamless shimmering of Time, where movement through Time itself encompasses what we once called 'movement through space.'

But if there's no space, *where is* this entirely temporal reality? Consider this: In the realm of dreams, the question of where the dream itself exists is not easily answered. It is neither in a specific physical location nor confined to any particular space. The dream simply is, resonating within the realm of consciousness. It is a fluid and ephemeral experience that defies conventional notions of spatial existence.

We could say, if we take a materialist perspective, the dream happens in the head of the human. But, now, from the point of view of the human, where is the universe?[5] It's not limited to a specific point in space or contained within any defined boundaries. The universe, in its vastness and complexity, transcends conventional notions of spatial location and is simply 'here and now.' It exists as a dynamic manifestation of Time itself and so *where* it is, is *when* it is: Here, and now.

---

5 The cosmic dream?

If we talk about locations such as here and there, we're talking about *relative* location. The cat is here and the dog is there. This is relative location both to each other and within a specified environment. Or saying, 'the dog is here, and the cat is not here' may translate *here* to mean 'life' or it may suggest that the cat is somewhere other than here - the specifics of which are unknown. This is all relative location.

So is there such a thing as *absolute* location? This is what the questions, "Where is the universe?" and "Where is the dream from the point of view of the dreamer?" are asking. The answer seems to be both no and yes.

No, there is no location that always exists as an empty void until something fills it. Such an idea would demand extensive explanations regarding boundaries, limits, external factors, potential edges, the spatial realm's existence, its duration, the permeation of time, and so forth. This line of inquiry generates more questions than answers, fostering contradiction, confusion, and impeding true understanding.

Yes, absolute location exists in the sense that whatever begins, appears in, out of and as the same infinite Being without exception. No thing can *be* outside of Being. Being however, is not *relative* and so has no location other than its own infinite Being - which is location-less because it's infinite. It is not *grounded* in Time. It creates Time and acts *as* Time.

If you imagine a planet that is entirely ocean, is the ocean in some place that is relative to waves on its surface? The question is nonsense; the ocean *is* the waves on its surface. It's only when we abstract the waves into independent entities that they can be in a location, but this location is purely relative to other waves. Attempting to establish their position relative to the ocean from which they arise is illogical. All waves, regardless of their size or form, are simply manifestations of the fluid and uninterrupted nature of the ocean. Location, is emergent.

In this same way, every location is relative and self-generated by the spontaneous appearance of Time. Any and all location is always *here*, but *here* is beyond relativity, it is infinite, eternal Being. Omnipresence.

Time, as finitude, begins where *it* begins and ends where *it* ends. The nature of Time is to begin, endure, and end.

Brahma, Vishnu, Shiva.

Creation, Preservation, Destruction.

The *context* of its appearance is timeless and location-less infinity. And so, in a playground of limitless freedom, Time is limitlessly and freely cycling, freely playing: 'Lila' - the play of the divine.

So we're not looking at a one-dimensional, linear view of time with three spatial dimensions in which it operates. Instead, we're looking at a three-dimensional view of Time as the self-same three-dimensions of space. Time, when seen in three-dimensions, is what an object is. Put another way, 'an object', is temporal process in three-dimensions.[6]

Therefore there is no 'matter' as distinct from Time; we have simply been imagining Time as separate from space because we are abstracting Time into a measurement. The 'linear change' we think about - past to future - is a mental tracking of the three-dimensional unfolding of Time into and out of infinity.

Look around you now as you substitute in your mind the three-dimensions of space for the three-dimensions of Time.

---

[6] The three dimensions (as the human way of perceiving eternity) serves as a means of explanation, but in principle, it is much more likely that Time unfolds into innumerable dimensions simultaneously.

Everything looks the same, but what you're seeing in front of you now is not objects in a space, moving through Time; you're seeing Time itself in three-dimensions, appearing to be objects. What a fabulous magic show!

By concentrating the three dimensions of Time, which can be equated to energy, in a dense region, we effectively increase the amount of Time within that space. Consequently, this region appears to endure for a longer duration compared to a less concentrated region.

From a relativistic standpoint, we can infer that regions with higher concentrations of Time experience a greater 'amount of Time,' while regions with lower concentrations exhibit a lesser amount. As a result, we would expect less concentrated regions to decay more rapidly, and more concentrated regions decay more slowly. This inference aligns with our broad observations: rocks endure longer than fruit, and stars far outlast human beings.

Here, I propose the Time-Energy Equivalency as another equivalence, akin to the previously established equivalences of electricity and magnetism or mass and energy. Rather than perceiving separate matter existing in spacetime, we view entities as Time-forms radiating their environment.

As Time radiates away from a time-form, it gives rise to the conventional notion of a 'spacetime environment.' Thus, it's not that a pre-existing fabric of spacetime bends and curves in the presence of energy; instead, time-energy itself serves as the origin point from which a creation of a spacetime gradient emerges from within. This gradient naturally leads to phenomena like time dilation, among others (see Application: Gravitation).

In this framework, one's perceived lifespan becomes relative to the proximity to a deeper concentration of Time. Observers closer to the core of this concentration would appear to live longer compared to those on the sparse and dissipated edges. Time on the periphery becomes thinly spread, fading into distant memories of its origin, while at the center, Time remains fresh, rich, and dense.

*

Past and future are relative terms, relative to a particular finite form. Being has no past or future, it is ever-present. Every time-form does not move towards some definite and concrete place called 'future', only its *own* future, and its own future is invariably: 'change until total dissolution'.

We may ask what it dissolves into. The future? But how could it? If it were to dissolve, it can only dissolve into eternity, into presence, because whenever it *does* dissolve, it must do so in the present. Therefore the past-to-future progression is a localised phenomenon, not an absolute truth.

It is worth noting that physical and mental phenomena share this characteristic. They appear, persist for a certain duration, and then change or disappear. The previous form ceases to exist as if it never was. Through memory, we can recall and reanimate these forms, but they do not exist in a designated place called 'the past'; they exist now, accessed and thought in the present. For example, dinosaurs are not living in the past; they exist now as birds, crocodiles, or even as fossils preserved in rocks.

All thoughts and memories of a past are illuminated in the present. If they were only illuminated in the future you'd never be aware of them simply because you cannot exist in your own future. You can only exist in your own presence and presence is, after all, the necessary nature of Being.

Nevertheless we do seem to experience what has been and gone, in the form we call memory. We can become aware of memories, pay attention to them, watch them and even analyse them by use of other memories. We can use this analysis to predict the way in which Time will unfold. It may be to do with stars and galaxies, it may be the behaviour of living organisms, it could be interactions of rocks; if you name it, we can ostensibly use memory to help predict what is not yet present.

This deeper inquiry into memory in particular, and the subsequent sense of individuality we assume from memory, is continued in the Application section. First however, let's continue our exploration of vibration and perception in order to establish a stable philosophical foundation before we leap into too much depth discussing the intricacies of how finite appearances appear to interact and their effects.

5

Quantum Mind Hypothesis

The quantum world presents numerous peculiar phenomena that defy common sense and the principles of classical physics. Bridging the gap between classical and quantum physics is a longstanding goal for many theoretical physicists. It represents the quest for a comprehensive "Theory of Everything" that can unite and explain the diverse behaviours of reality.

One of the fundamental issues as far as I see it, is the subject-object distinction and the nature of consciousness. Believing in a separation between subject and object, consciousness becomes an almost unbelievable facet of reality as it holds no shape or form whatsoever and has no location in physicality.

Quantum phenomena with their peculiarities and apparent contradictions, and the enigma of consciousness, may find greater coherence when seen with the lens of unity rather than fragmentation.

Let's investigate together.[7]

Virtual Particles

The idea of virtual particles proposes that energy in the form of two opposite particles can spontaneously begin to exist, only to annihilate one another a tiny fraction of a second later.

These particles are said to 'borrow' energy from the vacuum to begin to exist, and then 'give it back' on annihilation. Given that they share a common origin, they are also said to be entangled with one another. We'll go into entanglement a little later, but briefly, entanglement can occur when two 'things' come together and act like one system rather than two independent systems. Even if you sit in a room, your body is entangled with the room, and vice versa. If something happens to you, the room changes; if something happens to the room, you change.

Collapse Of The Wave Function & The Measurement Problem

The Schrödinger equation says that everything quantum can be described with a wave function (Ψ). The wave function itself is not observed because it is a mathematical tool, not a reality, but

---

[7] If you're interested in a more detailed explanation of the observations I'm about to describe, I recommend exploring books on quantum physics, watching related videos or perhaps attending public lectures. The following descriptions aim to capture the observations as accurately as possible within the scope of this book, without delving into extensive depth. However, it's important to note that this subject doesn't have a definitive 'answer' derived solely from the observations. The interpretation of quantum physics remains a subject of disagreement and diverse perspectives.

can demonstrate properties of both particles and waves. This wave function only represents *probabilities* of outcomes as opposed to the direct predictions of outcomes we can make in classical physics. A classical prediction might be: if the cannonball has mass y and has force z exerted upon it, it will travel distance x, arriving at time t. Many 'certainties' we could say. With quantum wave functions however, this isn't possible. Instead it is said something more akin to: there is probability x that particle y will be in location z, *when measured.*

Classical physics has, in its time, come to the philosophical stance called 'realism' precisely because it seems to be the case that objects and reality operate according to classical physical rules regardless of whether or not we measure them: our observation is inconsequential to the nature of 'objective' reality. This is realism. Unfortunately for classical physics, quantum physics seems to declare this philosophical position fundamentally inaccurate. Our measurements appear to be vital.

As an example, the behaviour of 'the electron' is best described with a wave function, a distribution of probabilities... until it's measured. If measured, it then has definite properties. It can be seen to act like a particle - a point of mass-energy. It seems like it can be 'found'. This 'finding' of an apparent object that was initially acting - for all intents and purposes - as a wave of pure probability, is an interesting moment. It seems as though, through measurement, a wave is converted into a particle.

This measurement of the wave function that converts wave to particle, probabilities to certainty, is the collapse of the wave function. The 'mechanism' by which a reality of sheer probability is converted into absolute certainty is mysterious and this is where we get into The Measurement Problem. The issue with the Schrödinger equation is that it tells you what is happening with a system only as long as you do not measure it. When you measure the system, it does not follow linearly from the equation - and that's a problem. Let's look at the double-slit experiment to demonstrate this more visually.

In this experiment, a stream of electrons is fired at a screen that has two slits in it that are very close together. Behind that screen there is a second, blank screen. When the electrons are fired at the double slit and the results are checked *after* the whole experiment is finished, the pattern on the second screen is an interference pattern.

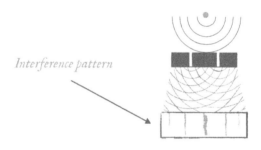

Interference pattern

This would be expected if *waves* went through both slits at the same time (illustration above). As the wave goes through the two slits, the peaks and troughs of the wave interfere with each other (hence the name of the pattern), cancelling out or amplifying itself at various intervals and so produce denser regions where they amplify and lighter regions where they cancel each other out. The electron therefore appears to be a wave, not a particle.

So what if we send only *one* electron through at a time? That way they wouldn't be able to interfere with each other and we can see, based on the back screen, how they're moving.

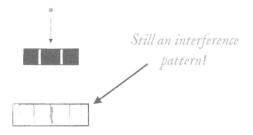

Still an interference pattern!

But it's still an interference pattern, potentially implying that it's interfering with *itself!* So is *each* electron going through *both* slits?

Clearly we don't fully understand something here. Well, what if we measure/observe the slits while the experiment takes place to see exactly what's happening? If a measurement is taken as the experiment unfolds (rather than afterwards), only firing one electron at a time, trying to observe exactly what happens at the two slits, then we see that the electron did indeed only go through one slit or the other. But here is where it gets *really* interesting. On the second screen, it now only displays two lines - as if particles went through, with no waves in sight.

As if particles went through the slits, not waves

Here we have observation/measurement 'collapsing the wave-function' - the wave-like nature of quantum probabilities has somehow turned into particle-like behaviour of classical physics. But even when observing it up close, right at the slit, there isn't any clear 'mechanism' that demonstrates *how* this happens. How probability is updated to be certainty. So from this it seems as though observation actually has a role to play in determining what reality *is*.

Perhaps in an attempt to maintain the idea of realism, there is another exclusively physical explanation called 'decoherence'. It goes a bit like this: In the first experiment that created an interference pattern, the wave structure of the electrons could be said to be "in phase" or "coherent". When waves are in phase they can interfere with each other as described above, and so produce interference patterns. However, when the electrons are observed as they pass through the slit they become entangled with the measurement device and so are shifted "out of phase" becoming *decoherent*. No longer able to interfere with itself it becomes particle-like, and so we begin to get classical physics, as quantum waves become classical objects.

The only issue with this is that it only theoretically removes the self-interference aspect of the wave function, but doesn't allow for a prediction of one definite result as in classical physics. It remains stuck in probabilities of one state or another, and so only partly solves the measurement problem. I know exactly where the cannonball will land or where the planet will be when I use classical physics, but we can't use classical physics when we filter quantum phenomena through the lens of decoherence because there is still no definite prediction possible. It remains in a mixed state of probabilities.

The measurement problem largely comes down to the measurement postulate, or, measurement update (same thing). After you've made a measurement you must 'update' the probability of what you have measured to one, or, 100%. It's a kind of cheat in a sense, because this absolute certainty doesn't follow from the reductionist view that is woven within quantum mechanics, neither does it follow from the Schrödinger equation. This update to one particular reality is something added in from a different theory of reality we have that is based on our senses. It seems that our senses do not detect a *probability* of a cat being alive or dead, our senses just seem to detect one or the other, a dead cat or a living cat.

To insert this extra bit, to update the wave-function probability to 1 only by use of pure observation without an objective mathematical mechanism, is pushing the limits of realism. Either there is a mechanism we do not yet understand that will help to maintain the view of an objective world that exists independent of our observation of it; or, observation *is* the mechanism we're missing that gives rise to matter and the physical world as we know it. But how can you turn observation into a mathematical quantity in order to sum it?

The issue with always looking for yet another physical mechanism is that we can always split one mechanism into two and ask what the mechanism is between those two new parts that make the larger mechanism operate. That's essentially what reductionism is, splitting everything in half and asking how the halves interact. But note that it always keeps the observer of this mechanism slyly out of the picture by simply never mentioning it. Quantum mechanics appears to be calling a halt to this, there is no more 'physics in a box'. The observer of the box must now be taken into consideration. This is what physicists wanted, a theory of everything; well, here's the opportunity to consider everything.

The Many Worlds Hypothesis looks to solve the measurement problem and maintain realism by arguing for - you guessed it - many worlds. In this hypothesis the Schrödinger equation, the wave-function, is believed to accurately represent physical reality - reality really *is* all possible states - and when the observation is made, reality itself splits into all the states represented by the wave-function and we simply discover which universe we live in. In this view there is no collapse of the wave function, instead, the universe as we know it splits or 'branches'.

It's quite an interesting take on it, but this still fails for two reasons. First because we don't observe all outcomes of the splitting universe and so the probability of the outcome still needs to be calculated in *this* branch of the universe, leading us straight back to the measurement update problem. Second, because it simply inserts an additional concept of a universe-splitting observer in-between the wave function and the measurement problem, as if delaying the measurement problem gets rid of it. The function/action of the measuring device/observer is to split the universe, but now we have to ask how observation does that. How can observation split reality in two? Where do these other realities exist? - Physically on top of each other; in the same place; next to each other; are they in a multiverse? What does a multiverse look like? Is it physical? Are there places where there aren't universes? How are they created? Where is the space? Was that space there before? Was it empty? We are just going up and up, escaping the question by trying to outrun it into other dimensions.

Another important interpretation is the Copenhagen interpretation, and it says that the wave function represents the knowledge an observer has about a system. This means the measurement update is necessary when a measurement is made because the knowledge of the observer changed. However, it shares a similar problem to the Many Worlds Hypothesis in that the distinction of an independent observer is also not fully congruent. How is it separate, especially, how is the observer - made of that which it observes - determining reality and collapsing the wave function? If there is an independent observer that has knowledge, and all we're representing is knowledge, why would observing an electron going through one slit or the other change the electron's behaviour? I don't doubt it has something to do with knowledge but there must be something more if simply observing something makes it act differently. If we cannot say anything about *how* it happens, then reductionism and realism suffer a heavy if not deadly blow. If figuring reality with finite quantities of tiny physical things leads us to a place where those tiny physical things seem to arise from an ocean of pure probability and possibility, then the fundamental view of a finite, 'building block' style existence is at best, inside-out.

So the question we're left with is a little misleading. It isn't simply about how the wave function collapses to only one outcome. It's a little more than that, and it focuses on the careful maintenance of the core belief of modern science: reductionism. The question is rather, "What is the physical and mathematical mechanism by which undetermined probability suddenly becomes determined outcome?" Having been lead so far for so long to this moment of the Schrödinger equation, a choice must be made. Do we go all the way back and look for a different line of thought to take that leads us away from this so as to preserve realism, or, do we discard our belief in realism and/or reductionism? It seems, on the weight of evidence, it may have to be the latter.

Discarding Realism

Only if everything comes out of the same basic principles will a theory be considered complete, or, solved. However, the theory has been conflated with the starting philosophy. The philosophy is a reductionist-realism, stating that physicality is real and is made of minuscule finite physical pieces or bits. What is the method by which we can determine the truth of this philosophy? The method is to observe the physical world declared to be the ultimate reality and, using experiments performed in and on that world, provide evidence for the claim that it is indeed ultimate reality. What better place to acquire evidence to support your claim than to rigorously investigate the claim itself? The trouble is, this claim reaches a moment where it points beyond its initial precepts and shows that there is something *else* at play.

The philosophy of realism has certainly brought massive advances in technology and has created a system of astonishing predictive power over physical systems, especially when we get to Einstein's theories and Quantum Mechanics. But now, having followed our curiosity in reductionism, we've discovered that the notion of an actual reality that exists independent of what or who observes it, no longer makes sense. Einstein said reality is relative to the observer, but I don't know if he quite envisaged just how relative it may actually be. It may in fact be *dependent* upon observation. So the physical sciences, dedicated to studying the nature of the finite appearances of reality, seem to be reaching their limit at what looks like the limit of physicality itself; a border that inexplicably evaporates into pure observation.

It is here that we must be prepared to discard the philosophical standpoint of 'objects as fundamental reality' and seek a new interpretation that doesn't have us struggling and clawing for ways to tape over the gaping holes appearing in it as we study existence. It makes no sense to cling to a clearly erroneous belief about existence when what we're looking for is the truth.

Entanglement

Without going into the intricate details of the experiments that demonstrate them, I'll simply summarise a few key points of entanglement. The details of the experiments can very easily be found online so if you're interested in knowing how this was discovered, the information is readily available there.

There are two key points, the first is that if two particles share a common origin - come from the same decaying energy source for example - then when we measure both of them along the same axis of measurement, they always produce opposite results. Let's say we measured for spin along the vertical plane, our result would be either 'spin up' or 'spin down' referring to the axis and rotation of spin.

Spin Up   *Spin Down*

If we only know the measurement of one of those particles, then we know immediately what the measurement of the other was. If the result was spin up, the other must have been spin down. This implies that if we only measure one of those particles here on Earth and the result is spin down, even if the other is two hundred million miles away, we know that it must have the property of spin up.

The common analogy is: if you put a left glove and right glove in separate boxes and send one to your friend, when she looks in the box and sees the left glove, she knows you have the right glove. It sounds analogous but it isn't, and that's to do with the wave function we talked about earlier. Just in the same way that the result of the double-slit experiment is a wave until it's measured/observed, the argument here is that in fact there is no 'spin up' particle that waits to be discovered, perfectly paired with a 'spin down' particle, also waiting to be discovered. Essentially, it does not even become a particle until it's measured, and when it is measured for spin like this, it takes on the property of spin up or down. This measurement seems to collapse the wave function at both ends, thus we collapse it here and simultaneously get a particle with the exact opposite property over there, two hundred million miles away...

Einstein was not cool with this. It seems to defy causality entirely because an instant communication appears to take place over distances that would require - according to his theories - time. Firm in the conviction that nothing can travel faster than light, 'hidden variables' were hypothesised to be present in the particles, removing the requirement for information to be transmitted between them instantly because all the information is already hidden within them.

John Stewart Bell created an experiment to test this and the result shows that any hidden variable hypothesis that is local to the particles (as Einstein thought it would be) must violate something called 'statistical independence.' If statistical independence is violated, it means that what a quantum particle does depends upon what is measured.

This seems to destroy realism because the awareness/observation/measurement appears to determine the nature of the physical world. The physical world comes from the observation; observation does not come from the physical world. Again, we may have had this whole thing inside out.

Now this is not saying that the moon would disappear if everyone on Earth shut their eyes. The processes going on out there in the solar system, the processes we call 'moon' for example, are consistently interacting with *everything else* that's going on. And this is where it is important that observation/awareness/measurement is seen as a natural function of the totality, of reality itself. It's not measurement with a ruler labelled with centimetres and inches to determine comparative properties, but measurement in terms of reality knowing itself via interaction. It doesn't mean ego as the foundation of course, as ego, equally, is something there is awareness *of.* So the atoms cascading from the 'stars' towards the 'moons' of the universe are collapsing infinite wave functions based upon their vibration and the awareness/observation that this vibration embodies. This creates relationships and interactions that, for particular senses evolved by peculiar little organisms on nearby planets, look like a star and a moon.

If there were no senses of this sort, there would be senses of a different sort. There may be aliens that do not observe infinity the way that humanity does and so what they interact with is not the matter we perceive. They may not see the moon as a ball of rock, but as something altogether incomprehensible to us. Perhaps they cannot see its outer layers as we can, and see only the light that is reflected. Perhaps they can mainly perceive electromagnetic fields as visual appearances and so don't see much of a star at all, but see stunning arcs of light and electricity! Only the scale of the imagination limits the possibilities. Looking laterally, even the perception we have of 'our mind' is simply another method of perceiving the same infinite reality.

So now let's return to wave function collapse. Does it collapse here and send information faster than light over there? It seems unlikely. The perception of any individualised or localised phenomenon requires by necessity the perception of something that is *not that* perception. If something is *here*, it cannot also be *there*. If you want to perceive light, you must simultaneously conceive of darkness. Congenitally blind humans have no notion of darkness because they have never experienced light. You only wander in darkness by comparison to having previously wandered in light.

If we collapse the wave function by measuring it either $+x$ or $-x$, it will inexorably result in both. If you measure a coin on a heads-tails basis, you'll see that a result of heads is simultaneously a result of 'not tails.' You couldn't measure a coin as made-up of only heads any more than you could encounter a human that was only her left side. So whether we try to measure spin up or spin down, left of right, collapsing the wave function by trying to perceive a dualistic outcome *necessitates* dualism. The entangled system truly is *one* system until it is ostensibly 'split' by the perception of finite opposites. Your body is neither left sided nor right sided until you say, "That is your left side!" and then you instantaneously have a right side. It isn't any great mystery as to how the perception of a left side of a human communicated instantaneously with the rest of itself to create a right side. The right side was created by the mind at the same moment the left side was.

So in like manner, by measuring for one of two opposites, the other is created at the same moment. The result of the spin up or down experiment is, at the moment, seen as random. You don't get spin up if you measure for spin up and spin down if you measure for spin down - as far as modern thinking permits us to speak about this. You measure either spin up or spin down in the same way you measure either heads or tails: 50% chance of either. When you measure the second particle, it isn't like measuring your friend's coin after you flipped heads - your friend may also get heads. Instead, the second particle will always be the opposite. So what this points to *could* be that there is some communication between the two. If when you flipped heads your friend always flipped tails and when you flipped tails they always flipped heads, that would seem extremely odd and you'd begin to think there was some communication going on between the coins. But when we recognise that the coin we're flipping in quantum mechanics is one complete system, one coin not two, we shouldn't really be surprised that we flip heads and do not flip tails at the same time.

In this way, it seems that to see the wave function for two variables as *one complete system* is imperative. The notion that one particle over here knows what one particle over there is doing and so updates its spin direction, is still falling into the same trap of finite appearances being actual finite realities - 'realism'. It is to say that the waves on the ocean are somehow independent from one another and from the ocean; that the waves form the ocean, not the ocean that forms the waves.

Is that satisfying enough for a scientific mind seeking a mechanism? - Maybe. The complication with a physical mechanism though, is that the tool of quantum mechanics - the wave-function - is the last moment of any possible information precisely because it says that we *cannot* know outcomes, only probabilities of outcomes. To then ask how any given probability physically turns into an actuality is to know outcomes not probabilities, thus denying the unreasonable effectiveness of quantum mechanics.

The belief that we can know how any given probability manifests into physical 'bits' is the same belief that quantum mechanics is, at the very least, 'incomplete' as Einstein suggested. This would mean either throwing the wave-function aside, or admitting that this is the limit of physical investigation and to complete the "Theory of Everything" we must begin to include the rest of the 'everything-ness' currently being sidelined i.e. mind and consciousness. To that end, we must ask if there are any parallels between the experience of mind and the observations of matter.

Virtual Particles & Spontaneous Thought

How is it that 'virtual particles' can appear spontaneously as a pair of opposites with shared energy, then annihilate one another and vanish? In the same manner, how is it that in our direct experience, thoughts can appear spontaneously out of nowhere as dualistic concepts (pairs of opposites) and then disappear again moments later?

We can't know exactly what thought we'll have thirty-seconds from now, but we might be able to make a prediction with some accuracy based on our current thought. Yet, by trying to predict it, you're now only thinking about what you think you *would* have been thinking about, had you not been thinking about it. Our observation of it changes it and we can't know what would've happened if we hadn't interfered.

The spontaneity of its appearance, the ambiguity of its origin, the ethereal nature of its tangibility, and a mysterious disappearance are relevant to the description of both virtual particles and thought.

When thoughts appear, they appear as a pair of opposites. The rising pair is both subject and object, and then dichotomies of objects. When the *object* of thought is annihilated, the *subject* as the experiencer of the that thought is *also* annihilated. That is why in sleep, when there are no thought objects, there is also no individual self experiencing the lack of experience. Virtual particles, like thoughts, arise as a perception of a division of unity. One may begin to conceive of virtual particles as if they were thoughts of the universe. And ultimately, all thoughts appear to be predicated on the question: "Am I divided?"

Entanglement & Recognition

The appearances of thought are often triggered through recognition (repeated cognition). What is happening now is referenced to some previous experience and a link is made between the present and the past.

One of the most interesting ways in which this presents itself in experience is through spontaneous and improvised prediction of something that grabs the immediate attention. An example is of this is the perception of danger.

Imagine yourself sitting under a tree on a sunny day and you notice a wasp flying closer to you.

Let's say you had a bad experience with wasps, you were stung once as a young child; it was frightening and quite painful. When you see a wasp in the present, that memory from all those years ago spontaneously appears in your experience as *two* events.[8] It appears as both the memory of it, and the future prediction based on the previous pattern: "It will sting me again unless I move away from it".

Now we have an interesting situation. We have a potential future event that we are aware of and a remembered past event that we are aware of, all taking place immediately in the present. We are experiencing, in the present, two entangled events separated by a distance of maybe twenty years.

20 years ago   *3 seconds from now*

Now

---

[8] Again the link to 'virtual particles'

If the memory wasn't present then the prediction of being stung by the wasp wouldn't be either; and, if the wasp was not present, the memory is equally unlikely to arise. As they share a common origin, past and future are entangled and information about one informs the other.

As past and future can only ever arise and decay in the present, it is the eternal immediacy of presence that gives the appearance of the two events 'communicating' with one another across a vast expanse of Time.

If the wasp comes closer to you, the energy builds between the past event of being stung and the future prediction of it happening again, as these events get closer to meeting one another. Spatial proximity is temporal proximity and so the closer the wasp gets, the closer the two events are to being in the *same* location as each other - colliding in the only place they can: the present.

If the future prediction meets the memory, the two annihilate one another and form a new memory made of both experiences; just like when two planets collide in an early solar system, creating a new, bigger planet.

As you are stung again, the energy built up between the two events is released in the present - perhaps in the form of a cry of fear and pain.

If the wasp simply flies away without stinging you, the energy between the two will dissipate and the prediction and the memory will subside gently back into the void from which they came.

Collapse Of The Ignorance Function

We can isolate anything in the mind and try to understand it. First there is one isolated example, and then we can learn more and more isolated instances of it. From these we can make connections and create a predicted pattern of unfolding, or if you like, predicted behaviour. We can apply this knowledge to 'the world' and we can see our predictions happening in 'real-time'.

Let's explore an example. Reading about a concept in this book is the observation of a collapsed wave-function, 'a static particle' in a sense. Imagining what it would be like in your everyday life as you read about it is an attempt to turn this particle of knowledge back into a wave; to reverse engineer it by attempting to predict its potential movement in a probabilistic way based on your previous context.

If the explanation I've given of any particular concept is an effective one, then witnessing it for yourself in real-time will enable you to clearly recognise similar looking 'static particles' that were pointed out in the explanation, while witnessing the continuous movement of the real-time display. Like screenshots taken from a video, or frames from a film.

The wisdom of experience can be likened to the ability to perceive a continuous flow of particle positions, transcending the need to rely on individual snapshots. It enables us to read the holistic movement of the wave function without requiring constant verification against learned particle positions. This new perspective naturally opens up a level of understanding unfathomable to particulate knowledge. When able to understand the wave in its totality, we can perceive both its continuous action - the wave - and its conceptual quantisation - the particle.

Let's take another more specific example.

When children are presented with static images or drawings of animals, such as a giraffe, they are encountering a simplified representation - a 'collapsed wave-function' - of something that is, in reality, an ongoing and dynamic process. However, when they witness a live giraffe, they are observing the wave in real-time as it walks, runs, moves, eats, looks right at them, and it blows their mind! They witness the wave, not the particle.

From this perspective, we use the particle to *symbolise* the wave; it is not the *truth* of the wave because the wave is not the static, collapsed particle. The 'particle' or image of the giraffe is the beginning phase of understanding because there is no such thing in nature as a static, unmoving, non-processional *object* independent of Time. That which is static is a symbol *representing* that which is non-symbolic and dynamic.

We seem to first learn about a process as if it *were* independent of Time, frozen, suspended, 'a *thing*'; then begin to understand it in terms of temporal process. When we divide the *entire* process of life into individual beings and things, we attempt to repeatedly collapse the wave-function of the totality in the name of knowledge. But then we miss a key aspect - the life. We make ourselves knowledgable of that which is neither dynamic nor alive (death one may argue), in exchange for ignorance of life.

The points, the particles, the 'bits' of information, the 'facts of knowledge' are isolated moments in eternity captured by memory. If we fixate on the position, the specific symbol, and cannot apply this discovery to lead us back to comprehending the total movement of the waving, the context, we have traded one ignorance for another. It's as if, in wondering what our own face looks like, we traded our south-facing chair for a north-facing chair believing we'll be able to see ourselves from this new angle. We missed something vital.

The Measurement Problem & Me

When attempting to explain the nature of existence in terms of physicality, specifically quantum physicality, we must acknowledge that both the object of measurement and the measuring device consist of quantum systems. They are inherently interconnected, as the measurement device is a constituent part of the experiment itself: the experimenter is made of the experiment. This reveals that human observers, being quantum systems, engage in the observation of other quantum systems, resulting in their collapse and subsequent experience of what the human system calls 'the world'. This implies that the quantum universe possesses the remarkable ability to observe and collapse *itself*, creating a self-observing and self-collapsing reality.

A complete quantum mechanical description of reality necessitates an explanation for how the quantum realm can observe itself and be aware of its own measurements. If all things are fundamentally comprised of quantum phenomena, then either consciousness itself, as the act of observation, is inherently quantum, or quantum phenomena is inherently conscious. The inclusion of consciousness becomes imperative in order to construct a comprehensive theory of everything.

The Observer made of the observed.

The observed, determined by the observer

If we consider an alternative to the ordinary interpretation of the measurement problem, we can view the measurement device (observer) as representing a quantum system it has entangled with, or indeed a quantum system it has *created* by the nature of its perception. Given that the observer is inherently made of what it is observing, every interaction is the quantum world manifesting at ever-compounding scales of perception spanning from pre-atomic interactions, to human perception and beyond. The vast scale of the universe emerges as an amplification of quantum phenomena achieved through its inherent self-observation.

It is crucial to acknowledge however, that the very notion of 'quantum phenomena' arises solely from the act of measurement, shaped by the nature of the measurement system itself, formed through prior observations and the collapse of wave functions.

This appears to imply a universe where an infinite regress of preceding quantum systems act as observers for subsequent systems to manifest. Within the framework of a mechanical cause-and-effect universe, this paradox limits its explanatory power. However, when we perceive reality as inherently conscious, the self-observation necessary for the compounding collapse and simultaneous expansion of the universe is the fundamental nature of reality itself: infinite consciousness.

In our everyday direct experience, 'measurement,' 'observation,' or 'perceiving' is not something conveyed to us secondhand by machines or the environment. It even goes beyond intellectual knowledge and instead embodies the essence of living itself. OBSERVATION IS THE VERY EXPERIENCE OF EXISTENCE. Niels Bohr himself said, "It is meaningless to assign reality to the universe in the absence of observation."

The awareness of the innumerable entangled states of Time's movements at this scale of existence gives rise to the experience and sensation we know as 'being human.' In a poetic sense, the totality, often referred to as God, is self-aware as a supposed separate entity. Some religions express this as "God became man," more directly however, we may say it is where absolute unity perceives itself as a state of separation.

There is now an alternative interpretation of the Many Worlds theory that offers further insights into the nature of the mind. Time is known through observation; our awareness brings forth the temporal world we perceive. When we cease observation, as in deep sleep, the world seemingly ceases to exist.

Drawing from the Many Worlds hypothesis, we can propose that the act of observing Time appears to split the unified fabric of existence, not into distinct physical worlds, but into something far more profound. The observation and belief in Time appear to fragment the indestructible unity of existence into the *perception* of opposites, into duality.

Through the observation of Time, we start perceiving dichotomies such as left and right, here and there, on and off, memory and prediction, past and future, life and death. When we identify with Time, we assert that we are Time itself. Consequently, our world becomes a realm of perceived separation. We witness the division between left and right, past and future, life and death, as fundamental schisms of the universe.

In this world of opposites, the newly created 'individual self' traverses a spacetime landscape, seeking a theory or interpretation of this fragmented reality that can reconcile and unify these opposing elements. We may turn to systems of organisation, like mathematics, in search of an equation that acts as a cosmic glue, binding these seemingly independent realities together.

However, as long as we perceive from the perspective of Time, from the finite vantage point, no glue is potent enough to unify the infinite array of dichotomies. Only when we shift our perspective to the infinite can we grasp the true nature of the finite. Only when we perceive from unity does separation dissolve. By perceiving the world as fundamentally divided, we become entranced by the illusion, oblivious to the fact that it is, in truth, undivided in even the slightest measure. To change our world, we must shift our perspective. Division is merely an appearance, a spell cast by the mind of Time.

What the investigation into the quantum realm seems to be doing is leading us to the conclusion that there is unity in all opposites. We can wait, postpone the inevitable and still dream of separation, creating more particles and more forces, but this mirage of Matter and Mind as separate is an illusion of Time. In reality, Matter is the tangible manifestation of Mind, and Mind is the introspective experience of Matter.

*

It seems implausible to uphold the belief that qualities of an objective reality are truly known through measurement, at least not without some degree of self-deception. The insights provided by quantum experiments support this view. It becomes evident that it's the nature of our perceptions that becomes known during the process of observation. We can only bring forth what we are *capable* of knowing, rather than capturing the entirety of what actually exists. If the essence of reality is eternal and infinite possibility, then it is our mode of perception that becomes the object of knowledge. What is perceived is, in fact, the very act of perceiving itself.

The process through which observation transforms infinite possibilities into perceived reality cannot be explained solely by physical systems, as it is the act of observation/awareness/consciousness itself that gives rise to physical reality. The realm of physical reality is the domain in which physical mechanisms can be comprehended, but the mechanism underlying the transformative power of observation transcends the limitations of the physical realm.

"The Universe looks more and more like a great thought, rather than a great machine."

- Sir James Jeans

6

Consciousness

As yet, in the world of objective scientific investigation, there is no evidence that clearly demonstrates exactly how consciousness is (or could be) produced by the physical. There are various hypotheses, but using the tools of ordinary scientific thought, no mechanism has been found that can produce consciousness as an effect of a cause.

It is absolutely true that by affecting certain areas of the brain, experiences and memories can be manipulated or destroyed. Psychedelics can change the experience, alcohol, food; many things can change the experiences we are able to have. Brain trauma can create amnesia and a total loss of experience and in some cases it can create new experiences never known before. Experiences such as being able to speak fluent French, or being able to play the piano like a concert pianist having never touched a piano before have been documented. This seems to imply the brain is more like an antenna tuning into different experiences it is capable of rather than purely down to the experience of any given life. But the correlation of brain activity to experience is only a discussion about the nature of experience, not about consciousness.

Thomas Nagel's essay '*What Is It Like To Be a Bat?*' attempts to make clear what is meant by consciousness by suggesting that it lies in understanding what it is *like* to be something. If there is anything it is *like* to be that thing, then it can be said to be conscious.

The question then arises: Is the fundamental awareness with which any experience is known different from person to person or species to species, or is it only the experiences that differ? The experience of being a human is vastly different from that of a bat, making it difficult to fully comprehend the experiential context of a bat. It is challenging for a human to imagine the context of a bat's experience, just as it's difficult to imagine a colour we cannot see. The experience of being a human involves the reception and interpretation of sense data, the storage and accessibility of memories, and other factors. The physiological and sensory differences between a bat and a human make it nearly impossible to precisely understand what it is like to be a bat from a human perspective.

However, it is worth considering whether the awareness of the experience of a bat, from the bat's perspective, would necessarily be different from the awareness of the experience of a human from a human perspective. Is the fundamental awareness with which any experience is known fundamentally different? Is awareness itself dependent on experience, or is experience dependent on awareness? Can experience exist *without* awareness?

The challenge in searching for consciousness within the biological brain is that awareness does not have a physical appearance or location; it is the act of looking itself. Awareness is subjective and holistic, and there is no specific part of the brain that, when stimulated, turns consciousness on or off. Altering the brain can change the experiences of which we are aware, but it does not imply that consciousness itself originates in the brain.

Bringing this into the context of death, the question is: Does the brain cease to produce consciousness, or does consciousness no longer experience the body?

Some argue that consciousness is merely an illusion created by physical processes. However, this position is wholly untenable because there is nothing illusory about being aware. Considering consciousness as an illusion or a hallucination raises the question of who or what perceives the illusion or hallucination. It leads to a paradoxical situation that cannot be resolved. If awareness is illusory, then what knows that it is an illusion? This line of reasoning is self-defeating.

It could be suggested that the illusion of being conscious appears to the body. However, this implies that the body is the knower of consciousness and is conscious of the illusion of being conscious, which is contradictory.

By labelling consciousness as an illusion or hallucination, we undermine our ability to deduce the nature of the physical world. If all perceptions are filtered through an illusion, then nothing perceived can be trusted to be real, as the medium and method of perception are themselves unreal. The endeavour to understand the physical world is rendered entirely pointless. Nothing that is perceived can be trusted to be real because the medium through and the method by which it is known is itself entirely unreal.

Consciousness must be actual because it is the only means by which any experience could be known and, it is sure that experience is known.

If anything were to be illusory, it seems that experience itself would be the most likely candidate, rather than awareness. Our perceptions are limited by the capabilities of our senses, which in turn limit the images and concepts our minds can conjure. Our understanding of the world is confined to the nature of our perceptions, and thus the world we perceive is a result of the human system's perception. It's important to note that the world perceived by a bat, for instance, is different from that perceived by a human, as each organism experiences its own unique world based on the nature of its senses.

Perceptions, emerging from the eternal sea of existence as it observes itself, play a role in co-creating the environment and the organism. Here, importantly, we have the beginnings of an alternate perspective of biological evolution.[9] While the underlying infinite reality remains the same, the way in which it is experienced is shaped by the nature of our senses and the filters through which we perceive it. It is this perception alone that we call 'the world' and truly, there is no *objective* world that exists independent of the perception of it.

It is only because awareness is, that these perception-worlds can be known. How could a world made of perceptions and interpretations prompt the emergence of the awareness of it? The senses function as the expansion of the aperture of awareness within an emerging world, and so it is in fact *the world* that is emergent within consciousness, not consciousness that is emergent within the world.

Senses devoid of awareness renders them redundant. However, consciousness can exist independently of the senses, as it persists in the absence of hearing or sight, for example.

So when I'm asking what consciousness is I'm not merely examining the physical processes seen when looking at memory, sensory impressions, likes and dislikes pertaining to different individuals; I am inquiring into the fundamental nature of being aware of all these phenomena.

Approaching this inquiry from an objective standpoint seems largely futile. We are investigating subjectivity, not objectivity. How can we objectively investigate something as

---

[9] Something that is expanded upon in Application: Evolution

inherently subjective as awareness? The more we emphasise objectivity, the less we truly explore subjectivity.

Indeed, when we say, "I was unaware of *x*," it signifies a lack of knowledge or familiarity with a particular thing. However, this doesn't indicate a change in awareness itself, but rather a specific circumstance in which we were not aware of certain aspects. Nonetheless, we remain aware, albeit of different circumstances. Therefore, I am referring to awareness not as mere 'knowledge of,' but as the fundamental knowingness underlying all experiences, including both knowledge and ignorance.

Just as we shouldn't mistake the light reflected off the moon for the ultimate source of light, we should also avoid confusing the illumination provided by thoughts or knowledge as the source of illumination for our experiences. Thoughts and knowledge are like the reflected light, they serve as intermediaries or reflections of the source, but they are not the direct origin of the illumination itself. The source of illumination in experience is the underlying awareness or consciousness that allows thoughts and knowledge to arise and be known. It is this awareness that illuminates all experiences, just as the source of light illuminates the moon.[10]

If we entertain the notion that consciousness may emerge from the entire body rather than just thoughts, we are essentially amplifying the belief that consciousness is a product of objects, albeit on a broader scale. However, we must expand our inquiry in tandem with the expanding idea.

---

[10] Much like how light is measured, we are only measuring consciousness via reflection. No one has measured the one-way speed of light, nor the source of consciousness.

Consider the Sun. What is it made of? It is made of its surrounding environment. Even though the environment appears pitch black, whatever it is, is in a sense what the Sun is composed of. There are no additional elements imported from another universe. It is akin to building a sandcastle on the beach using sand and water. Although the sandcastle may appear more structured than the raw materials, it would be illogical to claim that it's made of castles or castle-specific sand and water. It is nonsensical to suggest that the castle possesses capabilities beyond what the beach itself possesses. While the castle may assume a specific form, it remains inseparable from the beach.

Indeed, just as the sandcastle is an expression of the beach and cannot be separated from it, the Sun is a manifestation of its environment. The form and actions of the Sun are a direct result of the environment, and it does not possess independent capabilities beyond what the environment is capable of. The distinction between object and environment dissolves when we recognise that 'The Sun' is simply what the environment is capable of. It is a play of infinity.

Now let us turn our attention back to the body and consciousness. The body, being made of the environment, does not exist as a separate entity delivered from an external source, as there is no such thing as 'outside infinity.' Every action of the body is inherently the action and nature of the environment. So just as we may say that The Sun produces light, at a deeper understanding it is the nature of reality that appears to emit light and we name that concentrated point of light emission 'The Sun'. This same principle applies to the relationship between the human and consciousness. The human does not function as a *producer* of consciousness; rather, the human is fundamentally constituted *of* consciousness.

Consciousness is not a separate entity produced by the human; it is the bedrock of the human experience.

Consciousness must be an inherent aspect of Infinite Being precisely because it is present. Its actuality serves as undeniable evidence for its existence. If we base our understanding of reality on observations, we cannot deny the fundamental role played by consciousness in the process. Regardless of the location or characteristics of any alien being in the far reaches of the universe, if it possesses any form of awareness, it must do so with the same fundamental consciousness that underlies the nature of reality itself. While the alien's perception of the world may differ based on its unique senses, its fundamental awareness remains an intrinsic property of reality.[11]

Sometimes, in the investigation of consciousness, we may formulate the question "what *is it* that is conscious?" It shouldn't now make sense to say that the individual self is conscious because *that* self is a simulation. As Joscha Bach puts it: "It is a model the system makes about itself". This simulated self (the 'Me' - as discussed in more detail in the Application section under 'Memory') can be seen as such and subsequently lived without, yet consciousness remains.

It is therefore not the individual self that *does* anything because the individual self is an idea built around the body-

---

[11] In relation to the human organism, every other species, including plants, animals, and fungi, can be considered 'alien.' The goal of attempting to communicate with them is to strive for a better understanding of their world to enable us to communicate with them on their own terms. This is evident in the numerous books on body language for communicating with horses or dogs, for instance. The approach is to inquire about their world and how we can be attuned to it in order to effectively communicate needs and values in both directions.

mind phenomenon. It is not a *knower* of anything at all because it is what is known. It is like the moon's light. It appears to be a source of consciousness, but is really only reflecting the light of consciousness. The separate self, and indeed any mental object, is the experience of a reflection of immediate experience.

From the perspective of an ocean wave, the wave cannot conceptualise what the ocean is. If it tries, it can only do so in terms of finite waves - *uncountable amounts* of finite waves, and so the ocean seems divided. It remains confined to its own wave form and cannot become a different wave and therefore draws the conclusion that what it means to be the ocean is to be uncountable amounts of finite waves from the perspective of a single finite wave. No wonder it seems impossible and implausible.

So, is the ocean actually divided and separated because one wave cannot experience what it's like to be a different wave? The answer has to be no because it isn't a *thing* called a wave that experiences anything. From the perspective of the ocean, all waves are simply itself. The ocean alone experiences itself as waves here and there. The wave doesn't experience the multiplicity of the ocean, the ocean experiences the multiplicity of itself.

The same goes for the apparent distinction of bodies. Part of the structure of the body is this belief in separation. However, it is important to realise that the belief itself does not possess the capacity for experiencing. The belief *is* the experience.

The individual self is akin to a mental galaxy, comprised of interacting mental objects revolving around a perceived central entity known as 'Me.' However, upon introspection, when one investigates the center of experience, the 'Me' entity remains elusive. What is found upon closer examination? What is discovered when you look within?

In certain circles, it appears that Consciousness has been confused with experience. Matter, I maintain, does not *produce* Consciousness, but is an experience and manifestation *of* consciousness. In this sense, it's logical that the arrangement of molecules and atoms and so on will produce different and specific experiences according to their structure. Experiences such as a psychedelic trip, that of being a bat, a separate individual egoic center of reality and so on. A key mistake happens here - in identification with experiences if they were the limits and producers of consciousness.

Matter, Time, objects, they are all the activity of infinity and this infinity is self-aware. Any subsequent 'system of observation' is naturally aware because the movement is awareness itself - consciousness. This is not panpsychism - the idea that physical objects are realities unto themselves and they all 'have' consciousness as a property; this is unity, there is *only* Conscious-Infinite-Being, and Time is a pattern of its movement.

Each body therefore is not an origin point for the *creation* of consciousness nor a purely physical object that may *possess* consciousness. You are not a limited perspective that *has* consciousness; you *are* consciousness acting as a limited perspective.

In summary, the totality of Infinite Being gives rise to the manifestation of finitude, just as the entire universe's environment gives rise to the diversity of life on Earth. It is the same process without distinction. Conscious-Infinite-Being is what all of THIS is.

The illusory nature of the objective and subjective duality becomes evident when confronted with the absolute unity of reality. At its core, the perceived solidity of objects dissolves into a mirage, crafted by the symphony of countless interwoven processes. This symphony, the infinite dance of movement, embodies the essence of pure subjectivity - Consciousness itself. In this profound realisation, the need for the terms 'objective' and 'subjective' wanes, as they are merely relative markers on the continuum of experience. Thus, the paradoxical notion of absolute relativity unravels, unveiling the profound unity that permeates all existence.

The supposed realm of objectivity, by its very essence, remains confined within the boundaries of limitation, unable to extend into the infinite. The secret to its illusory nature lies in the nature of perception, obscuring the underlying truth that all is but a continuous process masquerading as solid forms. Subjectivity, on the other hand, has often been erroneously reduced to the realm of individualised responses to stimuli, neglecting its broader scope. By delving into the essence of subjectivity, we encounter consciousness itself - the infinite awareness that encompasses these unique reactions and perceptions. Even within the fluid realm of dreams, where responses constantly shift, consciousness remains as the unwavering thread connecting dream, waking, and sleep states.

Subjectivity transcends the realm of objectivity, unfettered by its apparent limitations. The perception of 'other' is only an experience. There is no actual other. There exists solely the boundless Conscious-Infinite-Being, and it is you. Embrace the profound realisation that you are indivisible from the fabric of existence itself, encompassing the timeless essence of both the present and the eternal. You are not separate from the world that surrounds you; rather, you *are* that which surrounds you, only localised. You are the awareness with which it is all known. You are the totality of eternity.

How could you ever be detached from the infinity of existence? How could you exist apart from the essence of Being itself? How could you claim to be devoid of consciousness?

You transcend the realm of concepts, for they arise from your very being. You are the very essence of what exists. You are synonymous with Being. You are infinity itself.

"I Am that I Am"

APPLICATION

7

Memory

KEY PRINCIPLES:
THREE-DIMENSIONAL TIME &
QUANTUM MIND HYPOTHESIS

It is peculiar how so many processes repeat themselves. Apple trees make more apple trees. After long enough, the fruit of those trees and the trees themselves may change so much that they no longer resembles the apples or trees we recognise; nevertheless it's still a similar pattern. A 'living thing' grows a seed of itself - only ever so slightly different - and that seed grows into a slightly different version of its parent. It's not so different it's unrecognisable - we don't get sheep being born from the blossom of an apple tree. There are clear patterns.

Process, Time, appears to be spontaneously self-patterning, completely self-organising. It does it without the need for an external director, or indeed direction, of any kind. After all, there is no 'external' to Being that could house such an entity.

We've already seen how patterns arise via observation, We've also seen how perceptions themselves are observed patterns. So how do they continue, repeat and cycle? How do these patterns end up as a star or a human or a tree? To explore this, we need to redefine our understanding of memory, just as we have done with time.

We ordinarily think of memory as something static, a preservation of a previous fact by physical processes and limited to brains - almost like a computer memory: the brain as a biological hard-drive.

Then there is the limitless field of consciousness into, out of, and as which these memories appear. When consciousness is modulating in a way so as to produce what we ordinarily call 'mental phenomena' such as images, words, ideas and so on, we can call this the 'dream-space.' The way memory operates in the human experience seems to be based on these two elements: stored experience, and the dream-space.

If you divert attention to the thoughts you have, you're accessing the dream space. If you watch attentively, you see quite quickly and quite clearly that there often isn't a choice as to which thoughts you have. You just witness the thoughts that are happening. In that sense, 'you' as a thinker of or possessor of those thoughts is no longer a tenable position. Any more than you can claim to own the wind. In a sense, you're watching the continuous involuntary processing of stored sense impressions, stored experience.[12]

What is called forth from storage depends upon the stimulus. The ink of this book can create a pattern that, through sense impression, is perceived and then referenced to other memories in the storage of the organism that are similar to the stimulus, and then images and information are conjured. Watch what happens to your experience as you read and perhaps linger on the words:

Elephant...

---

[12] We'll go into the *how* of storage in just a moment.

China...

Using language, which is simply visual and sonic pattern, we can manifest similar patterns in our dream-space. You may have thought of a cartoon elephant, a real one, maybe you've even seen an elephant with your own senses as opposed to through a recording. Maybe there's a smell associated with that experience. Maybe you had a sound or a movement of an elephant. Maybe it was a particularly striking picture you saw once. You may have thought of the country China. Maybe red dragons in new year festivals, maybe giant misty mountains, Chinese characters; maybe Kung Fu, maybe the flag, maybe you thought of bone china crockery.

The nature of the conjured experiences can vary from person to person, and can be images, sensations, emotions, and abstract concepts. Building on our exploration so far, we can extend this understanding to memories. If memories are not discrete objects, but instead are manifestations of process, then they too must be vibrations of some kind: the reverberations of past experiences. Memories emerge here as unique vibrational patterns within the complex orchestra of the organism.

Further, given that the particular vibrational patterns are brought about via observation and the nature of the system in observation determines the nature of what is observed, then the direct experience of different stimuli is different for each system, vibrational pattern, or organism. As a simple example, my experience of a sunny day will be different to yours because of the nature of our systems.

By recognising this relationship to the environment and begin to view memories as vibrational phenomena, we embrace the fluidity and interconnectedness of our experience. Memories are not fixed entities but ever-changing patterns that can be influenced, altered, and reinterpreted over time. It in fact necessitates this, as the more experience we have the more we are entangled with different vibrational patterns and so the interpretations of stimuli will necessarily be different to an earlier interpretation. What was once familiar may be seen from a different perspective, as the interplay between past experiences and present moments gives rise to fresh insights and understandings, altering the resonance of the vibrational pattern we call 'Me'.

Surrounding ourselves with a particular stimulus that conjures a particular feeling, image or otherwise, keeps those vibrations alive in us. Otherwise, we find that over time, vibrations will gently dissolve and disappear. This is why second languages need to be used to be maintained. It's also why we might cut out pictures of our heroes (or enemies) and stick them on our wall. These stimuli elicit in us a vibration, something we then interpret and describe as *a state of mind*. A state of mind we believe will help us achieve a particular goal. It may be Arnold Schwarzenegger on the wall of a bodybuilder, Lionel Messi on the wall of a would-be footballer, Marie Curie on the wall of a scientist daring to challenge the status quo. These goals are goals of feeling.

We use the stimulus to maintain a vibration within ourselves until we no longer need the stimulus because we *became* that vibration. Vibration perpetuated is resonance, resonance coming from the words *re* (again) and *sonare* (to sound): to sound again. Therefore to remember is to repeat a vibration, to 'sound it again,' to *resonate at that frequency*.

Let's take the understanding of 'eleven' as a quantity. We see some objects and are taught, "This is eleven. One, two, three..." and we learn that to count that many objects (stimulus) is 'eleven objects'. However, its important to understand that 'eleven' is not a reality but a linguistic representation of a particular perception. So when we encounter the word 'eleven,' whether in written or spoken form, the word acts as a magic spell and the sound, the vibration of the noise 'eleven' brings us into resonant harmony with the *feeling* we once had when we correctly matched the stimulus with the linguistic phrase associated with counting. The memory of 'eleven' is, therefore, the vibrational pattern or resonance enacted within the organism.

The *feeling* is what is remembered, the feeling is the knowledge. No abstract concept exists in the mind as distinct from a feeling, a vibrational resonance, of the moment when it was learned. Comfortable and loving, uncomfortable and fearful, and everything in-between and beyond, the resonance that harmonises with particular stimulus determines what are ordinarily called, 'likes and dislikes'.

So, it is the feeling that we call a fact, and then we use language to express the feeling. Just like we saw earlier when seconds are abstracted from observation and then we reify the 'seconds', here too we often mistakenly attribute the fact of the matter to the language used - "That *is* 'eleven'" - rather than to the feeling-resonant source.

Because the feeling is what's called upon with language, this is how words can upset us as they manifest in our experience. They are resonances that are disharmonious with our inherent nature. Jayne conjures up an image in Mary of Mary being something terrible (within Mary's context), and Mary then feels the terribleness of what it's like to know, or experience, that feeling in the context of her perceptions. Some phrases may not hurt Mary, but may hurt someone else; for example, hearing someone call them horrible might upset a person striving to be kind. It's not the language that carries knowledge, it's what the language symbolises. The symbol represents the feeling.

So memory operates as the subtle and profound ability to *resonate* at the frequency of a previous experience. Observation is then filtered through this resonance, altering the perception. Moreover, the perceived is affected by the perceiver, creating a loop of causality where two patterns of perception define and perpetuate one another.

If we consider mantra meditation, we can see that mantras act as focused phrases to cultivate a specific state of mind. Initially, repetition is used to reach this state, but eventually, a single utterance is enough to evoke the desired feeling. Mantras function like magic spells, shaping our inner experience. Similarly, the words we tell ourselves form mantras: "I'm strong" or "I'm unworthy." These phrases elicit particular feelings and can become long-lasting states of being. Some are friendly spells, while others are curses. For instance, the mantra "I am unworthy" acts as a curse.[13]

All this comes down to is resonance; a perpetual vibration of the time-form that you are, in a particular way. Resonate with generosity and kindness and you will *feel* the beauty of being generous and kind. This is why people say being good is its own reward. The vibration, the resonance, is so beautiful and harmonious that you really don't end up wanting anything else.

As a slight digression, morality takes an interesting path from here. Acting and feeling loving towards others benefits your own life immediately. While this can be seen as 'kindness is ultimately a selfish act,' its resonance simultaneously contributes to your own good *and* the greater good. As others perceive kindness, their own perception shifts towards kindness, creating a kinder world from within in each perceiver.

---

[13] I'd love to go into the folktales of witches as the villains casting curses on innocent villagers and the allegorical nature of these tales. Perhaps another time, as this would become quite a long but nevertheless very interesting digression.

On the contrary, acting with hostility and greed is entirely self-centred, spreading competition, fear, and disharmony. Morality doesn't require external laws from an external law giver; it self-organises. Acting amorally leads to a world of distress, while acting morally fosters a world of love and kindness for oneself and others. Morality is known innately by the feeling we have. Morality is then merely a label for the resonance of kindness, generosity, patience, equal treatment, and so on.

What all this could mean is that stored memory, what we might call long-term memory, is an ability to access a wealth of resonance patterns. A catalogue of ways in which the organism can vibrate to generate certain images or ideas, certain feelings, certain modes of thought, certain actions, and certain perspectives. We could say, 'memory textures consciousness'.

This is in no way limited to human beings, of course. Imagine a seagull flying back to its nest. It may be tired having flown all day and it's struggling to continue beating its wings. Why would it be flying back to its nest if its tired? What is its experience? This framework allows us to make a sensible estimate. Although we can be certain that it isn't thinking in English, Korean, Swahili, or any other *human* language, it is reasonable to say that the perception of the seagull is textured by the memories of feelings. Therefore, in this example it may be picturing its nest and with that is the feeling of comfort, warmth, rest and safety - exactly what it feels it needs. Thus, it moves towards its nest.

Being able to perpetuate particular vibrations is the ability to vibrate, resonate, in a similar way to how we did at the time of the initial experience. It is perhaps a reason for the human's increasingly bigger brain over time - not so that it can 'have consciousness' or be *more* conscious, but so that it can resonate with more variations of experience. This vastly increases knowledge potential as the organism can then combine even more experiences and be even more creative in the dream-space. If we remember only ten experiences we can combine all of them together, combine each of them with one another, combine the results of combination with other results, combine results with original experiences and so on. Adding even the capacity for one more experience to this compounding process would MASSIVELY increase the scope of potential understanding available to the organism.

With the recognition of remembered resonance however, comes the inevitable use of the dream-space for comparison between the present stimulus and what is remembered. This comparison can give rise to a dream-space backtracking through the vibrations in-between the present and the memory to arrive at a notion of a 'passage of time' between the two events. The gap is explained by the interplay of vibration patterns with one another, namely, 'Cause and Effect': Time's patterns conditioning its future movement, its future evolution.

We can see that even the type of music we listen to can directly affect the way we feel and so alter the way we interact with others and so alter the course of our lives. We also talk about a story or a song as 'moving' in reference to our emotions. Again we see that our environment can alter our resonance, and, in return, our resonance can alter our environment.

Epigenetics, the study of how life experiences can influence DNA expression, aligns with this perspective. This perspective implies that by interacting with specific vibrational patterns, the DNA (simply another vibrational pattern) can adapt and harmonise with external resonances. Just as equilibrium and harmony are natural for temporal phenomena, it is reasonable to expect interactions between vibration patterns to lead to mutual change and similarity - uplifting or otherwise.

In this context, the impact of trauma and conditioning extends beyond the individual, affecting the DNA and potentially being passed down to future generations. However, the encouraging truth is that our capacity for change is not limited. The very fact that trauma can alter us in the first place indicates that we are not bound to remain fixed in a particular state. We are dynamic beings, constantly evolving.

This has profound implications for many biological ideas. The theory of random mutation and natural selection is one hypothesis, but the idea that every experience in life shapes future evolution is quite another. This latter idea sees intelligence and response, where before, life was only perceived as mechanical and mistake-driven.[14]

The unfolding, vibrating, resonating nature of Time interacts with itself and in doing so, produces a complexity of resonance. This complexity of resonance appears perhaps as quarks, electrons, protons, neutrons, atoms, molecules, chemical compounds, RNA, DNA, proteins, cells, even organs, brains, bones, muscles, organisms. This is continued resonance pattern on multiple time scales, combining and compounding to produce what we call 'life'. But, we can see that there is no seam where material process *becomes* biological process, no join where 'stuff' *becomes* life. It is all the same process only with more and more complexity. It is *all* life. The stars and black holes are life. This is a living cosmos!

The experience of living is an orchestra of resonating patterns interacting with each other. We can say that DNA is 'biological memory' - differentiating it from 'intellectual memory' such as where you may have left your keys - but,

---

[14] Evolution is explored in greater depth in the Application section.

distinction and a creation of categories is unnecessary if we can understand what memory is as a whole. We're seeing here that *all* types of memory can be considered to be continuations of vibrational pattern. These vibrational patterns, these resonances, are what humans call 'information'. This information is exactly the same as, is a synonym for, knowledge. The memory of a given individual therefore, is a particular complex set of vibration patterns - known about through direct experience of those patterns - resonating as the body.

The ability to access certain memories is the unfathomably subtle ability TO VIBRATE IN TOTAL ALIGNMENT WITH THE PATTERN OF THAT INFORMATION. By 'remembering something,' the process of human vibrates in resonance with the experience of the past event and the human essentially orchestrates time by the activation of particular resonances and subsequent identification *with* that resonance.

There is no doubt then that the experience of the body, which is made of Time, brings with it the experience of psychology, of mind - the experience of memories, thoughts, interpretations, sensations and perceptions. So the mind is not something separate, but is intimately one with the body. The mind-body is an experience of Time. Time therefore not only has the function of energy or 'matter', but also - in accordance with the experience of every living human - necessarily has the function of Mind.

In vibration there are harmonics - overtones and undertones. There are harmonics with wavelengths so small and large that you will never hear them with your ears, yet you still may be able to perceive them. The Schumann Resonance (7.83Hz, the resonance of the Earth) cycles too low for human hearing, yet studies have been done that demonstrates its importance for mental stability and biological regulation. A machine that resonated at 7.83Hz (a "Schumann Simulator") was even put aboard spacecraft for the benefit of astronauts who suffered from its absence. So perhaps memory, as a vibration, also has harmonics; harmonics we might not realise the body reacts to because they are so prevalent throughout our experience - like the Schumann resonance.

Following this stream, it is interesting to see that studies have revealed intriguing findings on the effect of sound (music in particular) on water droplets. When exposed to Classical music, the droplets exhibit concentric and symmetrical patterns, while Metal music produces sharp and overlapping shapes. This observation highlights the impact of resonance on the physical structure of water, which constitutes a significant portion of our cells. In dream interpretation, water symbolises emotional states, with rough and aggressive bodies of water representing unease, anxiety, tension, and fear, while calm bodies of water signify tranquility. Considering these experiments and the symbolism of water, it only adds to the mounting evidence that the vibrations we encounter directly influence the resonance of the mind-body.

Taking this into account, it seems that dreams (day or night) are an example of the body *translating* vibration into symbolism in the form of mental images and words. Each body gives a unique interpretation, a unique translation of vibrations into the context of their unique experiences.

If we are unaware of the importance of vibration, we may also be unaware of how easy it is to empathise with someone else. It's simply a case of being close to them for long enough to feel the vibration they're resonating with. In that sense, empathy exposes you to someone else's vibration and, depending upon how your body makes sense of those vibrations, you may end up having similar thoughts. This is one explanation for how couples, or those very close with one another, will sometimes think the same things at the same time - they're resonating in harmony with one another.

Vibrations affecting DNA, affecting the emotional state, and acting as bridges between organisms, are not necessarily radical ideas. It's simply observation. These harmonics continue.

If vibrations are translated into verbal or imagistic thought (into symbolism) by the organism, then the connection and interrelation of the vibrations and symbols would be the creation of rationale and reason. The on-going mental monologue or image stream is not therefore an action done by an individual self, but an observation of the natural function of the body and even, reality itself. It is the communication of thoughts with one another; vibration patterns interacting with one another and the realm of the intellect translating those into symbols gives the experience of symbols chattering with symbols. It is relativity in action, relationship between resonances of experience, gently making 'sense' of experience. It is the work of the body to harmonise experience within itself and attempt to unify it into one cohesive notion that makes sense of as many vibrations as possible at once - ideally, all of them.

Making sense of something is to find harmony within the mind-body and with resonances external to its perceived boundaries. This change in resonant structure would naturally lead to a change in interpretation of the world by the organism, interpretation both of the new structure and of external vibrations. This change of interpretation is experienced as a change of mind. As the resonance of a Time-form like DNA, or the body as a whole, or indeed any Time-form, is simultaneously the resonance of Mind, to change one's mind is literally to change the material constitution of one's physicality

- even if only slightly. Traveling the world inevitably leads to a change of mind regarding some if not many ideas because direct physical experience of altered states of vibration, altered states of mind, are undeniable for that individual, and the healthiest thing for the organism to do is to accept the truth of experience to allow harmony.

If I experience transcendental states of consciousness, or the compassion of a loving human being, or the anger of a trapped human being, those resonances will relate to mine and one or both of us may see something new, and change. This is learning. Learning is therefore the natural way of Being - ever-evolving understanding. Of course, the new resonance can be resisted for many reasons, but it cannot be unexperienced. Until both the resistance and the new resonance are accepted, the individual is in a state of internal conflict, trying to resonate on too many different frequencies at once.

The old way of thinking is to see in only one dimension and say that the thoughts and emotions are produced by the body and pure physicality - even though there is a total lack of any explanation of exactly how mind 'emerges' from pure physicality. There is no need for such an arbitrary conclusion. In the new framework we're setting out in this book, it becomes reasonable to assert that certain vibrations and resonances of thought and emotion influence the body, while the nature of the body's resonance can shape the types of thoughts experienced.

Take a moment to observe the faces of older humans. You may notice that a lifetime of harbouring angry thoughts and experiencing anger has left its mark, contorting their lips and forehead into a closed and scrunched position. Conversely, a lifetime of cultivating joyful thoughts and experiencing happiness has moulded their facial features to be open and receptive. Simply observing older humans can reveal dominant emotions that have prevailed throughout their lives.

As an experiment, sit in a quiet place and watch the mind for ten minutes. If you don't get involved, don't identify, and don't interfere, but just watch, you will see that it is always changing - by itself. The mental processes of identification and belief determine whether or not a thought is merely a thought that will change, one of many transient experiences, or if a thought is 'truth' - the perception of some objective and permanent reality. Identity brings the *concept* of truth, but detachment brings the realisation of the truth of concepts. Emotions, stories and even belief are resonances capable of being observed.

Sometimes the question is asked as to why humans have emotions. Now we can see that this question is asked from the starting point of the intellect, often from a materialistic and survivalist perspective. Really the question put into the mathematical formulae creating machine of the intellect is, 'Why does the *intellect* need emotions?' Then the answer churned out is, 'To connect socially to enable survival'. Again we see how the perspective creates the world around it in its own image: "God created man in His own image."

If we look at it differently, we see that emotion is a primary perception of vibration. Emotion may be generated or accessed by a memory, or by a present event. From here we can inquire as to the link between the intellect and emotion and ask, 'Why do we have the intellect?' Now it seems clear that the particular intellect the human has been developed is useful insofar as direct experience can be translated into symbols and so communicated to others. By being able to communicate with others in this way we can, as a collective, explore the experience of being human together. In those moments, we essentially create a collective mind and can meet experiences with understanding, blowing open the doors to compassion and thus resolving disharmony, allowing a return back to the natural infinite unconditional love of reality.

The intellect is used to relate experiences of vibration to one another. But, without the vibration, the symbols are purely abstract. It's the vibration that gives a stimulus a feeling of reality.

*

When we cling to our comfort zone and avoid the unknown, we limit our experiences and perpetuate a cycle of familiarity and pleasure-seeking. Our predisposition to reject unfamiliar stimuli stems from a fear of potential harm, leading to a biased perception that reinforces our negative expectations. This process goes beyond cognitive bias; it involves the creation of our own destiny by unquestioningly relying on memory as the defining narrative of our lives. This perpetuates a repetitive history, known as 'samsara' in Buddhist and Hindu traditions.

The concept of projection comes into play here, extending beyond psychological phenomena. Just as time and vibration are interconnected, the resonance of our DNA, emotional states, and thoughts are themselves time-forms that radiate energy. The projection of the psychological realm aligns with the radiation of the physical realm. Our thoughts, emotions, and the vibration of our body-mind shape our perception and directly influence the environment, just as the environment affects our vibrational state.[15]

Therefore not just organisms, but every appearance of what we call objects, are like sentient mirrors - built of vibrational resonance. It is the universe reflecting itself back at itself. "Look," it says, "I am also *this* awesome thing!"

Time, Mind, and Body are all synonymous. The body is the accumulated resonances of the environment(s) it has lived in (both recently and through the billions of years before) and so is a concentration or 'crystallisation' of the totality on each and every scale from atom to galaxy and beyond.

A human is a concentration of the universal resonance of Being just as a giraffe is. However different human and giraffe seem to each other, they are very similar when we compare human and giraffe with The Sun or the planets. Yet, all are purely vibration and resonance of the universe, remembering itself in innumerable harmonics of vibration.

There is another, fascinating harmonic of memory that occurs - the scale on which it occurs is something I daren't guess. It seems that just as the there is a translation of vibration into emotions and emotions into acute thought-objects, the

---

[15] Even if you do not transform your environment with your 'projection,' until you stop resonating with that pattern of thought/emotion you cannot help but see the world as you are creating it, precisely because you are at the center of the distortion. The fabric and structure of your world is the nature of your resonance. Don't like your world? Change your resonance.

overall cohesive structure of the organism appears to translate all of the above into one big bundle called 'Me'. Then it tells a story about it.

'Me'mory

Isn't it peculiar that humans are often referred to as 'story-telling animals'? We casually engage in storytelling in our daily lives without questioning its significance. We weave narratives about mundane events, extraordinary discoveries, and personal struggles. But why? What is this inherent tendency to tell stories actually for?

From a Darwinian Evolutionist perspective, storytelling could be attributed to its social benefits for survival - a convenient explanation that avoids delving into deeper investigations.[16] Such an explanation is greatly limited and also fails to capture the elegance and expansiveness of the underlying reality. It seems to me that the reality must be much more elegant and much more expansive than such a limited worldview because, knowing that all is vibration and resonance of the same universal 'energy,' then what is so individual that it would be concerned with surviving indefinitely?

In order to look at this harmonic of the 'Me' (the individual self), let's investigate the way in which memory operates for world memory champions.

The most effective way for the majority of people to retain information in their memory is *not* through the isolated memorisation of individual dates and facts or relying on being born with a 'great memory'. If knowledge were actually compartmentalised and separated, devoid of any connections or relationships with other information, it would lack meaningful

---

[16] One could argue that this may be done out of fear...

context. We often overlook the fact that knowledge itself is not inherently meaningful; its significance emerges through its interconnectedness. Meaningful understanding arises from the relationships and connections between different pieces of information.

Your knowledge of how to use a spoon is meaningful relative to yoghurt or soup, relative to scooping things or holding things and so on. Knowledge is meaningful to us mainly through its APPLICATION; which is likely why many kids don't enjoy subjects in school that are not at the same time given a 'real world' application. There is no impetus to remember something that has no meaning because it is interpreted as literally useless. Precisely because memories mean things to us - symbolising something beyond themselves - is also how and why psychotherapy works, this is how and why dream interpretation makes sense of our emotional state. Humans are 'symbolic beings' because they are able to use symbols to represent vibrational experience. That's really all dream interpretation is: converting visual symbolism into logical understanding that can be connected to emotional states so we can better understand the experience of ourselves.

So, remembering each bit of knowledge with no relativity, like a computer hard drive for example, it sits inert, means nothing, represents no experience and has no other stimulus to react to that would cause its appearance. Isolated memory cells therefore - however many - likely will not be the way to general artificial intelligence.

In Richard R. Skemp's book *The Psychology of Learning Mathematics* he details a study carried out on the psychology of learning. They found that when learners had a relativistic schema of understanding, comprised of an interrelated set of concepts (compared to rote learning of individual, separate bits), learners were more than twice as likely to retain information to be recalled immediately; three times more likely to retain the information when recalled the next day; and over seven times more likely to retain information when recalled four weeks later.

A schema is a mental structure made of concepts that is from the first, routed in experiential understanding. The word 'blue' is learned as a concept by seeing and recognising 'blue' experiences, then abstracting 'blue' from experience into 'a colour'. Experience is abstracted; the abstract is never experienced.

The process of mental abstraction allows us to manipulate, combine, and categorise our experiences within the mind. Sometimes, due to limited information, these categories may overlap in ways that will cause later confusion. However, as we acquire more information, we discover new ways in which categories *can* intersect.

A young child, for instance, may initially perceive 'Daddy' as a tall man with a beard and short hair. Consequently, they may label anyone matching that description as 'Daddy.' The labels we assign through words represent concepts that are constructed based on sensory-based mental abstractions derived from our ongoing experiences. It is only through the introduction of additional mental categories that the child learns to differentiate and recognise that only a specific individual is referred to as 'Daddy.' In this case, the refinement of information occurs as the meaning and relationship to experience undergo changes.

Now let's reintroduce our world memory champions. If they can remember so effectively, then they must be using a schema, right? - Yes. So what is the nature of the schema of a world champion? What is the best method to use? The best method seems to be a story of an individual self, traveling on a specific journey through space and time. Objects that need to be remembered are put at landmarks along the way.

Red Roof:
Pick up kids

Lampost:
Lunch with Paul

Balcony:
haircut

Memory champions utilise a mental journey where they vividly recall landmarks and associate objects with each location. However, the key to effective memory retention goes beyond mere placement. It involves connecting the objects or information at each landmark with an emotional context, whether it be disgust, joy, stress, or any other emotion, it just has to make sense to the individual.

By gathering the organism's experiences into a cohesive entity known as "Me" and navigating it through the framework of "space and time" (even though they are not truly separate), memory becomes highly efficient. This split between self and the environment creates relativity and subsequently, meaning. In meaning is application, and the remembrance of useful and relative experience is what it comes to call 'knowledge'.

There exists here the idea of inherent meaning in the collection of memories that is termed 'an individual organism' precisely because the whole bundle *is* the application of relative meaning. This harmonic of memory that we call 'Me' the individual self, is therefore not the reconstitution of experience *by* an individual that would say, "I remember"; but is the reconstitution *of an individual in order to remember experience.* [17] The 'Me' is a simulated self in a simulated reality made of vibrational resonance that has been abstracted into objective symbols. It is the process of dreaming.

There is an experience of a 'Me,' but it isn't an entity at the center that remembers. The 'Me' appears, but I contend that it isn't an agent of action at all; it's a result of interaction and a means of recall. It isn't *independent* of the remembering, but a *function* of remembering.

The experience remembered and the separate 'Me' who supposedly experienced and remembers it arise together as the experience is understood in terms of relativity. This process is not evidence of an individual entity called a person; it is evidence only of the function of memory at a higher harmonic. It is the pattern of vibration *at this frequency* that is the creation of a 'Me' that supposedly enacts processes - just like The Sun supposedly enacts its own shine.

Humans frequently believe themselves to be individuals because the concept of 'a human' embodies the notion of individuality. To believe in it as oneself is to become it. The 'individual human' is a marvellous harmonic of cosmic vibration, but it is nevertheless a function of Time. It is a

---

[17] 'in order' can be read both: 'so that it is possible' and 'in appropriate sequence'. Both are applicable here.

mirage in vibration just like heat on the horizon appears as if water.

Reactivity

The creation of a story about an individual is a creation of a secondary, reactive vibration, a harmonic that is created relative to the first. The feeling being experienced can now be recalled later by means of resonating with the story of the 'Me'. Doing so will easily track stimuli that have been encountered and enable a search for a cause, a search for understanding relating to feelings and experiences. This is very helpful in the instance one is poisoned by a spider for example. What this implies is that the organism can become *attached* to feelings - good or bad - because they relate to the 'Me' it is identified with so that it can remember and so stay clear of fear and move towards joy, happiness, love and peace. Therefore, the organism will enjoy or suffer resonances and feelings in direct relation to how strong its attachment to identity is.

Gautama Siddhartha asked why we cling to suffering. Here it is, the clinging to suffering. It seems to be a process of fragmentation, division heavily assisting with recall. The more 'pieces' there are, the more pieces that can relate and resonate relative to other pieces. This means memories more likely to be recalled, giving them a higher chance to be understood and harmonised. As you have likely experienced with relief, understanding can annihilate suffering in an instant and reveal happiness.

Indeed, fragmentation can serve as a mechanism of fear. In fearful situations, fragmentation allows for the perception of escape from fear through actions such as fight, flight, freeze, or fawn. Fragmenting experience simplifies the application of information, enabling thoughts like "I, as an individual, can flee from this other individual if it poses a threat."

It is interesting to note that fear often emerges alongside sadness. It seems as if fear can act as a shield to protect the vulnerability inherent in sadness. However, if the fear of sadness becomes more significant than the actual experience of sadness itself, further fragmentation occurs. Experience becomes divided into a 'Me' separate from the sadness being felt, establishing a subject-object relationship. Moreover, a sense of 'Me' who is sad and an 'other' who is responsible for eliciting that sadness may also emerge.

Sadness is thus put at a distance from a 'self' and then reason and rationale join in with an attempt to explain how a separate object or event is affecting the separate subject or individual. This is a process of 'separation and bridge' rather than 'divide and dissolve'. The former maintains the perception of fragmentation and subject and object remain separate, though connected by a rope of reason named 'causality'. The latter dissolves separation entirely and all there is, is the universal vibration of sadness. What fear rarely sticks around long enough to find out, is that all appearances end eventually... including fear itself.

The deeper into fear and reason we hide our experiences, the further away from the fundamental resonance we go.[18] The simulated self, the 'Me' is thrown into a cascade of memories, seeking refuge from the overwhelming uncertainty by clinging to the familiar.

We often find comfort in what we already know, as it provides a sense of understanding. However, in moments of fear, we tend to ignore or deny the disharmony that may exist

---

[18] Can you see the same fear response of escape here? - Flight into the abstraction of reason.

between what we 'know' and the larger reality. It is unsettling to realise that hiding within the confines of a lie offers far less safety than embracing the truth.

When we listen more to fear than what the fear is reacting to, the fundamental resonance is avoided in favour of understanding a reactionary vibration - a fear-harmonic - of a conceptual individual who *is* sad. Sad about a particular thing, that thing itself fabricated with reason via the use of memories of what is already known: "I am only sad when x happens". Sadness, through fear, is now confined to specific condition x. Then, armed with a set of rational memories, sadness, pain and suffering are believed to be avoidable by evading remembered - and so known - *conditions* of sadness.

As undeniably clever as this would be for an organism living in environments riddled with potential causes of suffering such as being eaten by lions, bitten by snakes, stung by wasps and so on, this solution is only a temporary fix. Fear is enormously exhausting as it is a huge use of energy. Constantly translating experience into fear is bound to cause more harm than good. Acute trauma is something that can be recovered from, but chronic trauma - chronic fear - will become a disaster if left to continue, theoretically resulting in diseases, cancers and all sorts of illnesses as disharmony becomes the baseline of experience.

It appears as though the movement of fear, and the fragmentation it involves, seeks to break apart 'harmful' experience in hopes of dissolving it. This is the application of entropy to emotion by means of reason in an attempt to metabolise pain. But ironically and rather unfortunately, by fragmenting experience we turn it into rational memory and far from dissolving it, we maintain it. Look again, fear and survival go hand in hand here.

The way in which these experiences are maintained is often a cause of discomfort. What was once a whole and self-complete experience of an emotion is now fragmented, and the work of piecing it back together is even more distressing because it is a gradual return to the pain that was so intense at the time, you felt the need to escape it *through fragmentation*.

When piecing it all back together, it feels as though you're hurting yourself and if fear takes over again, there is yet another escape, which creates a *further* split. Now you might also be running away from any effort to resolve what you ran away from in the beginning: the fear of seeking help to resolve the fear of the event. It compounds. So by going to psychotherapy most are then brave by default.[19] Bravery does not seem to me to be absence of fear; bravery seems rather to be willingness to act in the interest of wellbeing despite the presence of fear.

We find, even if we don't piece the experience back together consciously, the fragmented experience is desperate to be resolved. Although it feels like we understand *why* we were sad, *why* we suffered, *why* we experienced pain, we do not actually understand sadness, or suffering or pain. The joke of it all is that the '*why*' has been entirely fabricated by cobbling together a bunch of old memories! The sense we made of it in the form of reason is only a story. The point of the story however was not just to tell it; is was created so that it could act as a landmark in the journey of the 'Me' through time to bring us back to the feeling so that we may return to it when we're able to face it.

---

[19] I say 'most' because it appears not everyone going to therapy goes for genuine help. Narcissists *may* simply go to improve their cultural image, for example.

This method, 'The Story' is nature's organic way of retaining resonance as a means of harmonising all experiences within one cohesive understanding of the totality. It creates wormholes that allow access to a resonance of existence previously experienced. In this way, joy, love, sadness, pain, any and every experience can permeate through time and be understood and experienced by later generations.

To understand a resonance of emotion in its totality means that sadness for example is not understood in terms of, or relative to, some condition. It doesn't result in an understanding such as "when *x,* then sadness". A total understanding is devoid of fragmentation and so devoid of conditions. It is not an understanding *in* Time, but an understanding *of* Time. What is understood is the movement, the vibration, the resonance of Sadness itself.

Just like we can identify the experiences of sound, sight, touch, taste, and smell, through total surrender to emotional resonance we can equally identify the movement of sadness. It is the same sadness that can be observed in varying intensities across all beings when they experience it. At this point, individual stories of sadness become less relevant because we can intuitively recognise sadness as a fundamental resonance of existence, akin to the recognition of smell or touch.

The ability to pick up on the resonance of particular emotions comes through an understanding and acceptance of them. Therefore the most empathetic humans would be those who have a deeper understanding of suffering by allowing themselves to feel the pain without running away from it.

There is interest here perhaps in 'mirror neurones' in the brain within the skull. These mirror neurones are points of reflection. Often people say, "That person makes me feel in such and such a way," deflated, happy, cheeky, serious and so on. This may be coming from you, or it may be a case of reflection; a case of empathy as you feel the resonance of the state of mind of another as yourself.

When resisted empathy can result in conflict, when accepted it results in peace and harmony. Resisting the empathy, a separation appears of 'they who are upsetting me' and 'I who does not want to be upset'. Further escape... more running. Accepting the empathy, two are brought together in understanding. One may help another dissolve the dissonance of resistance to a resonance within themselves. The recognition of mutual humanity, of 'you are not alone in this,' 'you are not in opposition'.

Misunderstanding breeds conflict, separation and duality, and so is usually dissonant. Understanding breeds equality and harmony. Understanding is acceptance without the least resistance. It is peaceful. Why else would fear escape into the known? When you are afraid, are you not in search of peace? Do ideas not come to you in that moment with the motivation of what would bring peace to your experience most effectively?

The problem is that this process is contradictory: Because there is a clinging to the known, to what has *already* been experienced, that usually brings a refusal of the unknown - a new experience. In that refusal there is an escape into what is known in an attempt to reach peace. But, believing peace is only found in what is known, fear of what is new plays a central role in life. Taken to the extreme, every new experience would be met with fear and escape back into the known. It's a temporary fix employed permanently and is no means towards lasting peace.

If there *is* resistance, this isn't a problem. It's natural. It's a moment of choice. You may resist walking off the edge of a cliff. This resistance is much more likely to maximise happiness in your life. But, you may resist being vulnerable, and this resistance is much more likely to isolate and alienate you.

Resistance is simply fear alerting the organism to something, like guidance towards happiness. It needs a moment to analyse and weigh up what is the best course of action. If you watch it within yourself, you find these moments are an opportunity to escape. So why would there be a drive to escape? It could only be down to the assumed 'facts' of The Story superimposed onto the present.

The Story of *who* we are is not fundamental to *what* we are. The Story is an effect, a *reaction* to resonance. To live exclusively from The Story, the rationale - which is built entirely of past experiences - is to live a second-hand life. It is to live in the present only through the lens of the past.

To remain in the care of the past is to remain dependent on the parent figure of tradition. It may well be exceptionally useful tradition, but how will we know for ourselves unless we stop using the intellect as a barrier, and dare to find out what happens by our own experience? A child has no choice but to do this. A newborn knows nothing of the world of tradition and *must* ask questions. A child begins its life learning by experience, curiously experimenting and investigating. Then at some point is sat in a dusty classroom, and merely *told* what is true.

Dare we be childish in this regard? Dare we step outside the pale of authority so that we may experience first hand the truth of reality beyond concept? Every moment, is an opportunity to live fully.

8

CONDITIONAL LIVING

The realm of separation, division and opposition, of 'me and you,' is necessarily the realm of conditions and the conditional: "If this, then that". It is world is a world of Cause & Effect. We see that condition X causes effect Y. We see this both physically and psychologically.

In physical conditions, cause and effect are easily identified, following the billiard-ball explanation as above: Newtonian Mechanics. In psychology, things are ostensibly more complex. Psychology involves motives, choices, and intentions, in other words, the mere notion of an action and not the action itself. However, as we've seen from the chapter on the Quantum Mind Hypothesis, the very observation of that psychological movement changes the system and thus has a direct effect on the unfolding of physical events. So its clear that not only can physical events cause psychological effects, but psychological events can also cause physical effects as observation compounds through reality. The phenomenon of the mind-body is a whole system and is not mind vs. body.

Causality serves as a useful tool in daily life, but it should not be mistaken as the ultimate foundation of reality. Be certain, reality does not exist *because* cause and effect is observed; rather, cause and effect *can be* observed within reality. The distinction is an important one. The former is identical to abstracting 'seconds' from observation, and then using the abstraction to redefine the observation so that the observation is a result of the abstracted rule. The 'rule' - whether it is a law of physics or otherwise - is an abstraction from a previous observation, but it is not itself the regulation to which reality must abide. The rule or law is a quantification of perception based on the human organism.

Believing that everything, including existence itself, is the result of previous causes leads to the ideology of a narrow, one-dimensional timeline and the entrapment of determinism. In this view, there is no room for the unconditional, except for the paradoxical unconditionally-conditional nature of reality. This realisation holds great significance precisely because it demonstrates how an argument *for* the finite nature of existence inevitably results in an argument *against* it, as we must endlessly posit previous causes in order to 'explain' the fact that reality seems to be here at all. To admit that this is what is happening is to say, "Existence is self-caused, self-creating - and eternally so - at every moment."

However, in the conditional view there is simply no room for true infinity because infinity is neither caused nor an effect of anything beyond itself. Consequently, we become unable to see the forest for the trees as the notion of infinity is dismissed as unreal and the world is fragmented into supposed fundamental components - particles that serve as agents of causation.

Assuming this worldview we generate so many more problems than solutions. In Rebirth we explored many of these challenges, but now let's shift our focus to how this impacts the way humans perceive themselves in relation to these 'others' that emerge from the belief in fundamental division.

Consider the scenario of a child who becomes frightened when faced with something startling and unexpected, such as the sound of shattering glass. We observe that the cause of the shattering glass leads to the effect of fear, suggesting a conditional relationship between the two. The child may cry out for, or run towards, whatever they believe is safety. We can therefore contemplate the belief that seeking solace from that fear, perhaps by finding comfort in the presence of a caregiver, is also then believed to be the cause of the effect love, peace, tranquility and safety.

This belief in love and peace as something *caused* by some external 'other' is the bedrock of dependency.[20] In fact, identifying with *what* we know rather than the knowing itself, we are dependent upon everything outside of ourselves to validate our existence. We come to depend on external sources to provide us with truth, conforming to the authority figures who claim to possess it. As Caesar famously declared, "Divide and conquer," and throughout history, societal structures have sought to divide and control the minds of individuals, protecting and elevating certain individuals over others. Consider why monarchs and nobles of the past desired power over others. Their desire for control arises from the fear and vulnerability they experience without it. However, what is often overlooked is that living with power over others creates an inherent imbalance. Despite the control they exert, history reveals that they are equally plagued by rebellions and uprisings. They are trapped in a conditional world governed by the principles of cause and effect, accepting this as the

---

[20] In the interest of demonstrating connections in this conceptual framework, see the last paragraph on page 32-33 before the break.

fundamental nature of reality. Ironically enough, in their quest to become the master of what they fear, they become enslaved by it. The notion of the external 'other' separate from themselves casts an ever-present shadow over their happiness.

In moments of fear, the world appears divided into opposing forces locked in competition. Fear can consume us, dominating our perception of reality. For young children with limited memories and a narrow sense of scale, fear becomes their entire world, as they lack the context to compare it to other experiences. When peace is resumed, the conditional view permeates the sense of tranquility, creating a sense of arrival from a previous state of fear. The presence of an 'other' - be it a caregiver, object, or something else - seems to be the cause of love and peace. At times, the 'other' is perceived as the very source of love and peace itself.

Is this truly the way it is? If we attribute the power of *causing* love and peace exclusively to the 'other,' it implies that neither we nor they possess it inherently. This raises the question: What was the initial cause of love and peace, and why? If we perceive others as the source of love and peace, we must inquire where they obtained it from. Was it from someone else? And then we find ourselves asking the same question repeatedly, delving deeper into an endless chain.[21] What, then, is the ultimate source? Perhaps the answer lies in a shift of perspective, a fresh way of framing our experiences.

The infinity of Being, by its very essence, embodies complete unity and oneness. This implies that there is no ultimate conflict between reality and any opposing force that can overpower or destroy it. While there may appear to be

---

[21] Again, the infinite regress rears its comical head amidst the perspective of finitude as fundamental.

conflicts among finite forms and ideas, they are all expressions of the same underlying unity engaged in a dance with itself. It is worth noting that the human body itself is a complex amalgamation of various organisms, such as mites and bacteria, coexisting in both conflict and harmony. The harmony of their apparent conflict is what we call 'the human organism'.

Conflict is natural, but it is an illusory conflict between objects that are fundamentally different patterns of the same universal Being. Ultimately, the essence of existence is unconditional and ever-present, it is peacefulness itself. This profound peace is experienced when we transcend the impositions of conditions, free from the notions of should and shouldn't, past and future, and simply abide in the natural state of effortless being. Humans that are labeled introverts often feel this peace when alone, hence the 'introverted' (inward turning) behaviour. This peacefulness is non-dependent it is 'self-shining,' and it is entirely natural. We need only allow ourselves to feel it.

Within unconditional Being, diverse experiences, including fear, arise as transient vibrational patterns of itself. When there is an identification with the illusion of separation, such as with fear, the thought emerges: "I *am* fear," or more commonly expressed as "I am afraid."

When one identifies with fear, a distinct sense of self, the 'Me,' arises. Again, this 'Me' is not an independent entity but a thought, entwined with fear and the function of memory. The experience of fear and the perception of an individual self experiencing it are inseparable sensations. Yet, when we lack understanding of this dynamic, we believe that the individual self is a concrete entity that experiences emotions separate from itself. This belief leads us to seek external stimuli or causes that can supposedly bring about the effect of happiness.

From the perspective of fear, love, peace, and happiness are seen as conditional, always dependent on specific conditions or circumstances. It is a curious role that fear plays, creating a split to help avoid dissolution at the hands of the other it just created, only to later dissolve *itself* in rest. And so, in a remarkable twist of belief, fear becomes the compass by which the world is to be navigated, and in doing so, simultaneously becomes that which it does not believe in: unconditional.

The spell of identification with fear can be shattered when we recognise it as a mere pattern of vibration, shifting its role from being the foundation of reality to becoming a manifestation within reality. It is akin to removing a virtual reality helmet and uncovering what has always been present, though seemingly obscured. Your true reality is not one of separation and attachment, but unconditional unity and so unconditional peace.

However, for most humans, this process of realisation is unfamiliar territory. Many find themselves trapped in a state where love, peace, and happiness appear to be caused and therefore conditional. Consequently, they spend their lives pursuing happiness as if it were solely external, a finite resource to be obtained.

Through prolonged observation of human behaviour, it's clear that there's an ongoing attempt to engineer love by following learned patterns of cause and effect. As a result, love is perceived as contingent upon circumstance, environment, and pre-requisites of character.[22]

However, if we believe that we must first satisfy *conditions* in order to receive *unconditional* love, we are deceiving ourselves.

---

[22] These three: circumstance, environment and pre-requisite are all encompassed simultaneously by the word 'condition' and its grammatical variants, routinely implying all meanings at once.

That which is unconditional must be present *regardless* of conditions, many or none, because it must be present *unconditionally.* Therefore it must be present now, and it must be present *as* what we are because what or who we are also cannot be a condition to that which is unconditional.

When we deeply internalise the belief in the conditional nature of love, we face a significant dilemma. It goes beyond feeling pressured to conform to certain standards or behavioural expectations. At its core, this worldview opens the door to the possibility that anyone, including ourselves, may be inherently incapable of meeting the conditions imposed upon love. It becomes a circus act, balancing on the knife-edge of acceptance.

If this belief of complete unworthiness is identified with, attached to, or held, wouldn't you imagine it would manifest as feelings of insecurity, anxiety and depression? - Accompanied by suicidal thoughts or intentions? An individual damns themselves to a world void of love, unwilling to give it to themselves and refusing it from others, seeing it as *their fault* that they are 'objectively' impossible to love... what else would follow? Don't these reactions make perfect sense? It's not *illness;* it's the natural result of being convinced that you are a separate object, unworthy of the totality. This is indeed a spurious idea of truth.

Recognising the falsehood of this belief and embracing a more expansive perspective can be transformative. It involves realising that our worthiness and capacity for love are not conditional upon external factors or judgments. We are intrinsically interconnected with the totality of existence, and love is our innate nature. By shifting our perspective and embracing this truth, we can begin to heal, cultivate self-compassion, and open ourselves to the abundance of love that surrounds us and, in the purest form of truth, *is* us.

Desire

As we grow up seeking love and peace from external sources as external causes, our only option is to trust desire to lead us there. We trust desire to help us reach love and peace so that we may receive, achieve or attain the external effects that are bestowed upon 'Me,' the individual.

Seeing this trap, Buddha tried to make it very clear that there is nothing to attain, nothing to achieve, and nothing to reach. In saying we must 'attain' peace by means of following desire, we tell ourselves that it is not present *now*. We define ourselves into a struggle towards an imagined future where it *would finally* be present, perpetuating the idea that love is, in actual fact, conditional.

In order to desire something, it can't already be the case, or at the very least, is believed not to be the case. If I'm caged, I desire freedom; but how could I desire freedom when I am already free, except through belief in the erroneous notion that I am not free? To desire freedom when already free is to create a prison for ourselves in the form of a conviction that we are other than what we are.

The object of desire will usually be laden with conditions that must first be met before we can have it. The anti-desire if you like - or simply the fear - of not getting what we want, is depicted as the ominous abyss into which we would inexorably plunge if we cannot hang onto the branch of desire that leads us to 'salvation.' It is as though damnation is an inevitable fate for those who fail to earn their deliverance.

Once more, we encounter the inherent authoritarian worldview that permeates this perspective: "The only source of happiness lies in the hands of the 'other' as the ultimate authority." In other words, "You are powerless."

It is indeed peculiar how we overlook the question of whether we can meet fear's conditions, convincing ourselves that fear has no conditions and is simply our natural state. While there is nothing *wrong* with this and it is our prerogative to hold such beliefs, it is an unnecessarily distressing perspective - one rooted in division and suffering as the fundamental essence of existence - while also being incongruent with observation and logical reasoning.

When fear and suffering are perceived as inherent and unalterable aspects of existence, our world becomes one characterised by struggle, hardship, conflict, and the constant pursuit of survival through competition. Happiness, in this view, becomes reduced to a mere chemical reaction, a temporary release of neurotransmitters serving the organism's survival drive. It raises the question: For what purpose do we continue to strive? Is it solely to seek the next dopamine rush? Is desire only there to guide a divided self to illusory reprieve? How deeply entrenched in fear and suffering must one be to believe that evading or conquering death is the fundamental motive behind the continuation of life? Reflecting on this philosophy of survival and conflict as the basis of life reveals the inherent absurdity of such a perspective.

Does it not make more sense to you that fear is conditional, and that love, peace and happiness are what is unconditional? Fear is after all directly related to conditions. One of the clearest examples is relief. Relief comes when believing something terrible has happened or will happen, only to have that belief proved inaccurate. The proof of the inaccuracy of the pattern matching process removes the fear in an instant and reveals what was behind it: peace.

In that same vein, chronic anxiety is the belief that many, many conditions are a cause for suffering and so you find yourself perpetually afraid. This is sometimes mixed with a resistance to the conditional fears being proved wrong - perhaps because being wrong is also seen as frightening. In this moment, there really is nowhere to go that is peaceful. Anxiety is completely understandable from the point of view of suffering and fear being conditional and so finite.

If we swapped it around, putting fear as the unconditional, we'd see that the extent to which one is happy is the extent to which one is ignorant of the truth of reality. How can this be reconciled with the living truth that after experiencing suffering, we later learn from it, accept it and return to happiness? We consistently return to happiness after learning. Suffering may be a current we flow though in life, but it does not make sense with the experience of life itself that it would be the sole makeup of our existence.

Therefore, it seems more coherent and congruent with our experience to view love, peace, and happiness as fundamental and unconditional aspects of being, while recognising that fear and suffering are conditioned responses that can be transformed through understanding, learning, and the realisation of truth.[23]

---

[23] This relates strongly to the coming chapter 'Evolution.'

Unfolding From Unworthiness

Fear gives rise to all types of other emotions of course such as anger, hate, resentment, disgust and so on. I use fear because, in the perception of conditions, it seems that the primal reaction is being afraid that peace, love and happiness has been taken away from us and in that, we can become afraid that we may be unworthy or unable to fulfil the conditions to return to it. It seems to me at least, that feeling unworthy of love (from others or from ourselves) is the most fundamental obstacle to unconditional love, created by the perception of a conditional world.

Thus we begin to look to memory for help. Memory holds knowledge of past patterns and may be able to figure out how to satisfy the conditions so that we may be happy again in the future. But, since there is a casting of the attention to memory, there is necessarily the function of memory - the phantasm of the separate self 'Me,' and the conditions this self lives in. The 'Me' is defined as unworthy from the outset. We become separated, fragmented and divided against ourselves. We do not see that we seek what we are! But, hypnotised by the dancing movements of mind, we forget this, and desire to *cause* peacefulness through action - or as the Buddhists say, through 'doing'.

Therefore, we see the human mimicking the parents, copying behaviours from role models - or from anyone who seems to have some of what is desired. We learn what to do and what not to do in order to satisfy the perceived conditions, of unconditional love.

This conditioning of the unconditional, I propose, provides a basis for understanding almost all human behaviour that is not loving and peaceful.

To immediately challenge this notion, there are individuals who appear to hold a strong conviction that love is unattainable for them, which leads them to actively seek situations that cause physical or psychological *harm*. At first glance, this behaviour may appear counter-intuitive. Why would someone willingly subject themselves to pain?

As we discussed earlier, the interplay between physical events and the psychological experience is evident. When certain physical events become associated with one another, they can create a chain of resonance within memory. This chain, interpreted as a thought-based narrative ("The Story"), shapes the individual's perception of reality. In the case of those seeking pain, their narrative is not perceived as a falsehood but rather as an accurate reflection of their existence: "I deserve suffering because I am not worthy of love." It is an application of self-punishment carried out automatically, conforming to standards imposed upon them by others. It is a habit, or, a practice of suffering.

Practicing anything will build up a mental strength in that area. If you practice the piano, you are likely to have the strength of reading music, understanding music theory and being able to find notes on the keyboard with ease. You could eventually do this without much thought as all the processing required to create new pathways in the neural network has already been done. The effort that began as a psychological intention becomes manifest as the effect of a physical increase of brain neurones relating to that area of repeated/practiced action.

The liveware that is the brain can be moulded and adapted based on perspective and outlook, experience, skills, and practice. Bearing that in mind, if you tell yourself your whole life that you are worthless and deserve pain and sadness, all the while confirming it in physical experience and action, you will build up strength in that area. That mental strength will turn into physical manifestations of that practiced behaviour. The more you rehearse the same story, the stronger the pathways get; the stronger the pathways, the easier it is for energy to run down that path and so you are more likely to run that path as opposed to any other. It is literally making the MOST sense in terms of pure quantity, and so appears to be the quality, the substance, of life.

It takes actual energy-burning effort to create new pathways to see the world differently. But the conundrum is, if you believe you're worthless, not just think it now and again but believe it to be *truth*, where is the incentive to use your energy to help yourself when you've deemed yourself unworthy of the result? This is the pitfall of depression. Pride may offer a branch, but it *will* let you fall...

So where are we trying to get to by creating all these pathways? When we run patterns of thought, what is the goal? It seems to be an effort to understand the nature of relationship. Patterns of memory resonance are combined and compared to make sense of experience. So unless we're open to exploring new areas of the mind, of the world, then all we'll be able to do is make the exact same sense of it... over and over again.

If these patterns of thought are strong we tend to have lots of experiential evidence for them. We experience something, interpret it through this lens, then rationalise it afterwards, further backing it up. At the next opportunity, we reflect on our rationale, run the same pathway, and then once again make the same sense of it. It can, at some point, even become distressing just to hear someone else fail to agree with the opinion we have. When it gets distressing, this is a sign of clinging too tight to ideas. Too tight simply means there is dependency upon certain ideas to provide us with a sense of safety - peace. But all *this* notion of peace is built upon, is aligning the resonance of the body with a particular *idea* of the resonance of the environment. If the idea is that the environment is abusive, aligning oneself essentially means to conform as something to be abused, thus bringing an adulterated form of peace.

For this individual, disagreeing with the idea of abuse can then be interpreted as a direct threat of our safety and in that scenario we are thrown into fight, flight, freeze or fawn and can become dangerous to ourselves and others around us. This is, more or less, the definition of Stockholm Syndrome, and is something worth paying attention to.

So much of our sense of the world is based in the habit of running the same pathways of interpretation in accordance with much of our memory, making them harder to challenge and breakdown. Nevertheless, just like if you stop eating the right things and stop exercising your muscles you're going to lose them, the same is true of thought patterns. If we stop feeding ourselves with stories of unworthiness, and stop exercising the mind by running the same thought patterns of unworthiness, then over time, the strength of the path will wither and the connections will fade.

Funnelling experience through the limited, narrow alleyway of a neural-narrative means we necessarily make sense of life in one way and not another. We say, "Life is thus!" because it is true for us, it is quite obviously the case due to the abundance of evidence from memory and the back-catalogue of interpretation. Again, there is nothing *wrong* with this, just see that it has the potential to create and compound suffering. The important thing is simply to understand the consequences of believing in it entirely. Regardless of facades, no one would choose suffering if they felt they had an option. Watch the patterns of your own mind as you go about your day. Are *you* inadvertently choosing suffering? You have the option.

By identifying ourselves solely with the interpretation of the world shaped by the our environment, we condition ourselves to feel free and at peace only when the conditions of that specific interpretation are met. We allow the narrative of what is deemed acceptable or unacceptable to define the boundaries of our lives.

By reflecting on the vast differences in human culture across the globe we can see that the likelihood of having particular conditions increases and decreases depending upon where you grow up. If you grow up in Iran your conditions are this, in Nigeria they are that, in Japan they're the other. Despite where we grow up however, it is always only us that permit our unconditional loving and peaceful nature to be limited, and the belief in and subsequent experience of the individual self - a particular interpretation of conditional life - is such a limitation.

Skinner's Pigeons

When talking about conditional behaviour, it's important, I feel, to mention B.F. Skinner. Skinner put pigeons into cages along with a device that gave out food at random intervals. He noticed that after they received the food, the pigeons were able to reflect upon their action prior to the food's arrival. They would then repeat that action again and again in an attempt to make more food appear. The pigeons couldn't see that the food came randomly and their behaviour had nothing to do with *when* it arrived. It was seen as mere superstition in the pigeons and a mark of low intelligence.

Here, this view blinds us to a deeper insight.

It seems to me that the result of this experiment demonstrates that pigeons (however lowly they are made to seem) act on the same belief of cause and effect that many humans do. What the randomness of the machine represents is the unfathomable complexity of any given situation. Therefore, although it seems sensible to apply memory of previous experience to a new situation, sometimes the action taken will do nothing to change the outcome, or may appear to have changed the outcome even though it didn't.

Every time the machine distributed the food, the situation became anew as the distribution intervals were random. Nevertheless, the pigeon, while acting from memory, was unable to detect the randomness, believing its actions to directly cause the desired outcome. The pigeons were attempting to create the conditions, through their actions based on memory, in an attempt to bring back the experience of satisfaction - realised in the consumption of food.

The extent to which the mind is able to transcend this trap is the extent to which the mind can see a bigger picture. It can remove itself from immediate pleasures by seeing their immediate transiency. In essence, the element of doubt can lead to deeper, or more overarching harmonics of truth.

Doubt leads away from the stimulus temporarily to 'take a step back'. Full knowledge of the stimulus may even lead to total abandonment of it as a condition to happiness. We may see that the conditions we are believing we're satisfying in order to bring about what we desire is not worth the effort; or further, will not in fact bring it about at all. It is seen as unnecessary to continue to create and uphold these conditions to our happiness, and so they are dropped. We may still engage in the activity and have fun with it, but the dependency on it is lost.

Isn't social media a technological example of treating humans a little like Skinner's pigeons? Each scroll brings the user a hit of dopamine and so the mind is lead to believe a dissonance. It believes both 'I am doing this action that brings the good feeling' and 'it is providing me with the good feeling if I do the right action'. This immediate pleasure transiency cycle can form a dependency, simultaneously reducing attention span, further entrenching the dependency on this method of satisfaction.

Strangely, the organism projects its own internal action of chemical production (in this case) onto a medium or media, as if the result were coming *from* the external environment. Integrating machine into organics in this way is the beginnings of cyborg-humanity, but, more extensively, this may not be the progress that was envisioned with the convenience of machines. It's turning out to be the continuation and in fact amplification of suffering as unconditional love is even further abstracted behind a paywall of more and more social and mechanical conditions that must be satisfied first.

Humanity feeds itself on the promise of more as it identifies itself with its desires. Desires being cravings of things that are believed to bring peace, they are conditions. "When I win the league, then I'll be happy," "When I get the car," "When I get the house, the guy, the girl, the new game, the bank balance". It's all projection into the future and a definition of that peace and happiness as not being present now. It may not feel present now. It may feel rough and uneasy. It may feel agitated and fearful. It may feel many things but peace does not seem to be present.

So lets look at what happens when a desire is fulfilled, let's jump right to the 'good bit' of the desire cycle.

When a desire is fulfilled the anxiety about whether or not you'll have it vanishes, because you *do* have it. The desire for this external thing becoming internal, that is, becoming *you*, is satisfied through proximity to it, allowing either identification with it or consumption of it.[24] This is the dissolution of desire.[25]

When the desire collapses there is no longer the thought that we should be someone else, be anywhere else, or do anything else. We are right where we are and that is perfect. There is peace. However, this might not last very long. The habit of external validation and gratification can be so strong that a new fanciful desire can begin *as* the previous desire is being satisfied. In this scenario, the satisfaction, the peace, is not fully lived in favour of picking the next desire so that it can bring us 'more' peace.

The joke is, if we simply did whatever we were doing in total involvement and appreciation, we could experience the depth of what it is like to be peaceful always, even amidst desire.

If you look at it in your own experience, you'll notice that the peace we return to on the dissolution of desire doesn't actually go away. It's only because new and different desires appear in experience, and with them the false assumption that because there is desire it MUST be satisfied, that it appears as if that peace has left. Try it next time you want something and get it. Sit in the peace of that without distraction. Recognise the feeling. When or if it happens, watch the rising pull of desire. Watch it create a magic show of need, of wish, of hunger and longing. Watch it put the peace you already have, at the end of some journey or another.

---

[24] It is easy to see how desire can drive an early search for food.

[25] If my desire was to be the best, when I hold the trophy I identify with what it symbolises because I am in possession of it: Rarely is it, "I have the championship," it's usually, "I *am* the champion".

You'll come to see that it is possible to recognise desires such as needing to drink or eat, and fulfil them in the total unconditional peace that is believed only to occur afterwards. It is the tension and unease indicative of a desire that feels like a lacking within the self as experience is dichotomised into subject and object: the subject who wants, and the object that gives.

If the peace revealed after satisfying a desire is linked with being an effect of a cause, peace is abstracted and becomes unstable. Then we lurch into dependency on that particular cause, which is an error, or rather, a misapprehension. Peace or happiness or unconditional love is not actually *in* a chocolate bar, or another partner, or a bigger house. We just believe it is, and so erect - for ourselves - conditions upon the satisfaction of which we will allow ourselves to feel peace and love. This really is the point.

We extend peace and love into the future as the greatest motivator we could possibly have. So when we say, 'the ends justify the means', we need to be very careful because the end is already present. The means may in fact just be making it more difficult to see that.

It may be all very well to read about it here, but is it a little too abstract? Can you see from this alone the conditional actions in ourselves that we take, imagining it will bring peace and love quicker if we do? Is it possible to see our defensive actions as we attempt to protect that which we feel leads us to happiness? Is it possible to *see* our aggressive actions that try to prevent others from infringing upon our happiness? Can you live from the perspective that perceives much of what humans do - their behavioural habits - as having been picked up as ways to satisfy the 'correct' conditions to avoid suffering and move towards acceptance, understanding, love, peace and happiness?

My question is, why all the reactivity? Why the: "Don't you DARE talk to *me* that way!" Why act it all out?

9

The Human Performance

Humans may want to be firemen or actors or to have a pizza this evening, but when it really comes down to the most important thing, it is ultimately to be loved and to love, unconditionally. You may not believe it exists, is impossible, or some kind of fairy tale, but it doesn't stop the yearning for the peacefulness of being unconditionally loved and of unconditionally being love itself, radiating from the inside out.

Love, in this context, extends far beyond lust, sex, or physical attraction. While sex can be an expression of unconditional love, it can also be driven by desire, jealousy, anger, or aggression, often stemming from a lack of love, as saddening as that is. Sex is not the center of love, nor is it the source.

The word 'love' has been commodified by modern society, often associated with material gifts, romantic dates, or confined to the realm of romantic partnerships. However, love flourishes not only between two or more individuals in various forms of relationships, but also when alone in transcendent self-realisation.

As we saw before, it is in the 'relating' of one to another that a separation is known and this can happen between individuals and within oneself. In this separation, standards, expectations and rules - conditions - hover in judgment over the best way to return to unity and love. They become goal posts; once met or followed, loving attention is given by the other as a reward. When the standards are not met this leads to punishments in the form of anger, resentment, cold-shoulder, and so on. Love can thus be experienced as conditional in romantic relationship or within ourselves. When the conditions are 'right,' love is present, when they are 'wrong,' love is not present - the standards of what is considered right and wrong differing with every relationship.

It's undeniable that effective communication plays a crucial role in relationships, as the absence of communication can create a barrier between individuals. However, some relationships can persist based on the belief that conditional love, characterised by separation and pain, is the essence of love itself. This is the mindset that declares that love hurts.

Unfortunately, the idea that love hurts is evidently false. It's *never* love that hurts; it's the perceived absence of love that hurts. Heartbreak is not love hurting you; heartbreak is the worldview that love has gone away - potentially forever.[26] It's the mix of loss and fear that hurts, especially when compared to the love felt before, seen through reflection. What heartbreak misleadingly suggests is that love is inherently conditional. Therefore, it is more accurate to say that heartbreak hurts, which is far less surprising.

Conditions In Childhood

---

[26] A break from (living from) the heart: heartbreak.

No one likes the idea that love is conditional, it feels incongruent, yet many stick to it while dissonantly believing that unconditional love is possible. In my experience, many humans can't shake this feeling that love is somehow, some way, actually and truly, unconditional. It feels like a truth beyond reason.

Now, that isn't evidence, but it's a good starting point. If we do hold the belief that love is conditional, we're necessarily sad about it on some level. By constraining ourselves within a framework of instability and limitation, we perceive love as fleeting and elusive. Increased belief in love's conditional nature intensifies fear and therefore diminishes the experience of love and peace. Then the 'saviour complex' often arises whereby someone will assume the role of the messiah, hoping to bring back the love that was almost lost, often, mistakenly, by use of violence.

The perspective of conditional love is often engendered by childhood experiences and early learning. Children possess remarkable capacity for learning, as every experience is new. An extremely significant transition and learning experience occurs during birth, which can be seen as a metaphorical death of the perception of the inseparable 'mother-baby organism' (to which the baby knows no 'outside') and the emergence of the perception of division: the 'individual baby organism' and 'individual mother organism.' This shift represents a separation from oneness to duality, from a state of undivided unity to the recognition of self and other. It marks the beginning of perceiving oneself as a distinct individual separate from others.

Reuniting with the mother's heartbeat as the baby is placed on her chest immediately after birth would ostensibly allow for a sense of oneness to return, perhaps because it is an opportunity for a reflection by the newborn upon the resonant memory felt in the womb, a resonance perhaps associated with safety. Like all epics and stories, it is the beginning that sets the tone for the whole journey. This splitting and reuniting will be the theme of the lifetime of the human.

After seeing the supposed split in parturition, the first condition might be: "Self in proximity to other is oneness." When self is in proximity to other, there are no longer any conditions because there is no longer any feeling of division. It's as it was in the womb. There is an immense opportunity for the mother here to witness that life is coming through her and out of her and so she is a portal, a source of incarnation, an origin point from which the enteral may manifest. If the mother sees herself instead as mother and baby, she won't feel the oneness of the two. The baby possibly thinks of two, but I believe it's much more likely that the baby in fact has no concept of two, of self and other. There is nothing that could hint that it was not growing directly out of and *as,* eternal life. This lack of division is Unconditional Love. It radiates, shines, and glows naturally when there is the absence of condition - the absence, of division.

We all know this absence of division, we return to it every night in deep sleep. The world of division dissolves as if it never was, and we're happy about it. If sleep were fundamentally anything else, such as resting in eternal fear and suffering, we'd wake up terrified every morning. There would be no such thing as rest, only temporary ignorance of fear and dread. Knowledge and understanding would then actually be considered a *threat* to wellbeing. To remain ignorant would be to remain healthy. Logically this would imply that life itself is entirely the escape of reality into ignorance of its own true nature - that of fear and dread. Life becomes an *escape* from truth not an *expression of* truth.[27]

However, learning is the natural action of life. Understanding is the natural way of things, and why would life seek comprehension of itself and its environment if it did not ultimately lead to a proliferation of wellbeing? Quite simply, it would not.

Returning to children, if there is a perception of a split, of distance, there is fear and then young children (and many other animals) will close this perceived gap by crying out. This little condition of distance as division is the seed in the mind that sprouts into an enormous tree of conditional living. Hunger may set in and discomfort appears. All of a sudden, a full stomach becomes a condition of peace in addition to proximity. Hydration, enough sleep, gentle sounds and so on and so on. Conditions pile up and multiply with each other.

Soon, the child may realise intuitively that proximity to other as a condition to unconditional love is self-defeating. Unconditional love is not present in the specific act of proximity because proximity to other is a condition. That is *conditional* love. Feeling its own radiant love, the child becomes curious. The toddler is prone to wondering off, prone to exploration! Perhaps now begins a journey of independent love. Only, in so many instances, the lesson is not truly learnt. Sure, proximity to MOTHER may have been transcended, but proximity to AN other often isn't as the child is given conditions and rules as to what is acceptable: "don't eat soil," "don't cry," "don't walk away!" The search is on for that *thing* that allows

---

[27] As one example of this worldview of 'life as suffering' and this 'escape from a reality too difficult to face' is seen manifesting in society through addiction, as humans try to remain ignorant of their experience by dependency upon some 'other' to help them feel better.

permanent access to what is felt as truly unconditional love - always available.

This desire can easily be transferred onto objects, later onto possessions, onto a partner, onto offspring, other's offspring, experiences, religious figures, music... Transferred onto anything perceived as 'external' to the self: something that accepts them fully, unconditionally.

Through an initial perception of division and the ensuing creation of a divided identity, the human is confused into undertaking a paradoxical search for its own dissolution into total unity at the hands of a separate other, in order to be at peace, all the while hoping to maintain its own survival as a separate individual. The identity, built of conditions and ideas of division, is also the desire to posses or 'have' the lack of division while still maintaining itself. Clearly this is an impossibility. A division cannot *own* oneness of everything, so it cannot 'have' this peace. True unconditional peace cannot be possessed like an object. It is found by recognising and aligning with the interconnectedness that already exists.

A wave cannot have the ocean, the ocean has waves.

When this search is transferred onto material objects, it implies an accumulation and a holding. The retention of these objects is, I contend, an attempt to retain the presence of the unconditional. If someone has not seen the futility of personal ownership abundance in the search for unconditional love, letting go of possessions or giving them away is not an option, letting go becomes counter-intuitive.

The story goes: it is easier for a camel to get through the eye of a needle than for a rich man to enter into the kingdom of heaven. In this context, a 'rich man' may simply be a human lost in the mistaken belief that accumulation of objects is the way to peace, to unconditional love - which is the kingdom of heaven.

Once you start down that road, every additional object, penny, or cent, only takes you further away from realising that a conditional view of life can never lead to the unconditional. You would be - literally in the sense of money - becoming more and more *invested* in a life built around satisfying conditions to happiness: "If I do this, *then* happiness, *then* peace..." There are *no* 'bad things'. If and when they're depended upon to provide unconditional love however, they do become... inauspicious.

Let it be clear, the unconditional peace of Being (which is love, which is happiness) is *unconditional.* It is present regardless of condition, in every condition, *as* every perceived condition. It is the natural, ever-present state of everything that is. It is total harmony even amidst apparent chaos. It radiates qualities seen by a conditional perspective as virtuous such as compassion, forgiveness, gratitude and so on, but it is not these things. These definitions and distinctions of character are reflections on the surface of conditional mind. Compassion is gratitude, gratitude is forgiveness, forgiveness is mercy, generosity is patience, patience is gratitude, forgiveness is compassion, and so on and so on. All virtues are one; they are the unconditional when met with different conditions.

Patience, for example, when viewed as a limited and conditional quality, transforms into mere waiting. True patience, however, transcends limitations and temporality. These temporal reflections of the unconditional are like imagining the entire ocean could be crammed into one wave. The ocean appears to be a wave, but it is only the temporal figuring mind that says so.

'Sins' are said to be the opposites of these 'virtues', but likewise aren't the many sins all one sin? Sin needn't be a means to beat oneself up, that's just compounding misery. Instead, reframe it using a broader horizon of knowledge. The detection of a 'sin' can instead be used as a guidepost. Sins can be viewed as indicators of movement away from unconditional love and into a life of conditions.

For example, naturally, conditions seem to produce actions seen as wrath, greed, gluttony, pride, envy, lust, sloth and many more. Again, these are not *evil* doings, they're just very clear examples of behaviours seen in humans who hold the belief in love as conditional. These kinds of 'sin' therefore, will send you to a 'hell' of consistent conflict and pursuit. But it's not hell in terms of an eternal afterlife of a given human, but a reality of life *now*.

By acting with greed, pride and wrath, your life changes all around you and it becomes 'hell'. You might feel you must battle and fight and maim and kill if you wish to stay alive in hell. On the other hand, giving up those conditional behaviours, letting go of the barriers and defences and acting with patience, gratitude and compassion brings you to living heaven. You needn't die to arrive in the kingdom of heaven; the kingdom of heaven is within you, it is your natural self.

Sins often have future negative consequences, which may begin to show a link between the Hindu concept of 'Karma' and the Christian concept of 'Sinning'. Overeating into obesity is an example of gluttony and has long been known to be a sign of seeking peace in consumption. But as we know, gluttony only leads to ill health for the individual.

This method of finding peace is a never-ending cycle of dependency. Those who look for comfort in sex also find that lust is unable to sustain itself. Those who look for it in elevating their ego to accumulate the sense of pride also find that it is a never-ending cycle of dependency, and of pleasure and pain.

No method that operates under the pretence of unconditional love being the result of satisfying particular conditions will EVER succeed in *giving you* unconditional love. The only success it could have, is in showing you that fact.

The idea that a particular object, person, action, etc., will give us what we truly want is a formulation of the mind. The creation of a simulated reality in which there is an attempt to figure out the correct pattern of behaviour that leads the subject 'Me' to the perceived object 'unconditional love'.

The pattern of conditions is simple at first and becomes more complex as parent/authority figures use a system of reward and punishment to train us to act in particular ways that are desirable for the parent/authority figure.

Material goods like toys, sweet foods, experiences, freedoms, and physical attention and affection are used as both rewards and punishments for obeying or rebelling against the standards, expectations and rules of the parent/authority figure. Often the removal of them is the punishment, or even just the removal of the *promise* of a future reward, such as Santa's naughty list.

The reward is often something a child will enjoy and feel peaceful around, thus the child begins to associate certain conditions - in terms of both standards of behaviour and environmental factors - with the arrival of peace and the 'return' of unconditional love.

The instability of abstracting unconditional peace and love like this comes from then trying to replicate the *image* of peace held in memory by reenactment of the perceived cause - like Skinner's pigeons. Peace is abstracted into a conditional response to a particular action or set of actions, and so naturally there is an attempt to perform that/those actions to manifest it for ourselves.

This is blameless ignorance of the understanding that there is no need in satisfying conditions to return to the unconditional. It is the belief that one must satisfy conditions to be at peace, be happy, and be in love. Even *with* these conditions and beliefs, you are not separate from Being. You *are* Being. It is literally impossible for you to be anything else.

Depression

This is what I wish to make abundantly clear so that we may break free from this cycle: Our own conditions to our love are why we do not feel unconditional love.

In the case of depression, the conditions to self-love (given by external stimulus) have been identified with and internalised. Looking at them is upsetting because the conclusion is 'I am not worthy of love,' but the deepest feeling is in opposition to this rationale: I *am* worthy of love. But isn't this the basis of every conflict? - Who is or is not worthy of love...? Isn't competition just the competition for who is the *most* worthy of unconditional love?[28]

If there is no one on the 'external' side of depression who is capable of understanding, who is a loving, caring, compassionate and patient presence, then the fight is on both fronts at once. The impatience and insistence to be 'well' immediately (or at least quickly) is ignoring the fact that the conditions found in the external environment are what has brought about the 'un-wellness' in the first place. A continuation of or an increase of those conditions will only lead to more depression - more turning inwards and so a further turning away from the external. Regrettably this can sometimes lead to more stringent rules and conditions to tighten control in order to 'fix' someone rather than listen to, accept, and

---

[28] There are some interesting thoughts on immortality here if you have interest to investigate that emerging conversational branch.

understand. Thus depression can manifest with self-isolation - MOVEMENT AWAY FROM CONDITIONS.

The anger, non-acceptance and stigma from the external world at the turning in, may in fact be because the human with depression is no longer able to give their love to others in the same way. As they look to give love to themselves, the conditions of other people's 'unconditional love' are being jeopardised.

If, in depression, the attack felt from the internal conditions is too hard to face, and the external environment is too hostile, there is an instance that invokes the desire for death; suicide. Suicide is the very logical conclusion to feeling as if *everywhere* is unsafe. But why? Why is death seen as more peaceful than life in this case? Perhaps for the same reason that sleep is known by us as peaceful. There is no friction, no desire, no conflict, no others. There is total peace. We feel better for having had a long and deep sleep.

The increase of depression in common culture does not, I maintain, demonstrate a lacking of character in a given generation, nor a need to increase medication potency. It is more likely demonstrating a lack of care by those in place precisely to provide that care. As a corollary, the increase of depression represents an ignorance of how current cultural conditions affect the heart of humanity.

The corruption of democracy in combination with competitive capitalist ideals generate laws and policies that lead to the degradation of compassion, the expansion of greed, and the maturation of the inherent alienation of individualism through separation and conflict. If we imagine humanity as an organism, this kind of behaviour towards yourself won't encourage the proliferation of love and peace. It is a system built around and for the continuation of war, both internal and external.

Depression is a recognition of this within ourselves, a natural super-power. It is the call of the unconditional to return home, to address the conditions that obstruct love. This reframing of depression is vital for transcendent wellbeing of whole populations. The necessity of more or stronger medication however, is merely a necessity of companies invested in chemicals to help them expand financially, not for the ultimate wellbeing of humanity.

Depression is nature's symptom of a society misguided. Patience and understanding is its medication, and unconditional love is the all clear. Psilocybin research into depression and the experience of deep meditation bring such remarkable results because, as I see it, they lift the veil on the conditional game of ego, demonstrating the reality of unconditional love present as the nature of existence itself.

Realising that love is unconditional, you see that you are not only worthy of it, but that you *are* that self-same love; and you are *always* that.

The symptoms of depression are difficult to miss. They can however be ignored or denied depending on whether or not there is a willingness to face one's own upset. Being unwilling to face our own upset often comes out by denying others *their* upset: by resisting it. If we wish to end suffering and expand a culture of love, we must begin to take responsibility for our actions in creating conditions for ourselves and others.

Trauma I

Traditionally, humans have held the belief that physicality is of utmost importance, neglecting the profound connection between mind and matter. However, should we dare to broaden our perspective and recognise that mind is inherent in the material process and vice versa, we can unveil the profound truth that physical conditions are a reflection of the state of mind. Through careful observation of the physical condition, we can gain insight into the mind state. This transcends mere intellectual thoughts, and finds truth in the material state of anything we can observe such as stars, trees and birds. For now however, let us focus on the human expression.

As we saw in Conditional Living, we can see a reciprocal relationship between mental and physical conditions. Mental states give rise to physical manifestations, which in turn reciprocally influence the mind. The idea that these two are separate is based on nothing more than an arbitrary belief. Traumatic experiences therefore can be held in the physical body as mental tension.

For this reason, it is my current view that when trauma is experienced and it remains unresolved, it acts as a condition to love. The fear, held as tension, blocks acceptance and one is left in a state of self-abnegation and surrounded by self-criticism regarding those key issues associated with the trauma.

Traumas appear to play a significant role in the construction and fortification of our strongest neural pathways. They serve as poignant landmarks within the narrative of our lives, often telling stories about ourselves that we would rather not confront. In their unresolved state, they persist within us, until they can be deciphered, thus perpetuating the pain. This sheds light on the childhood traumas focused around being subjected to confusing and frightening circumstances, and then facing punishment for seeking understanding about them. These experiences leave us grappling with a complex web of distressing conditions around remaining ignorant of the pain we feel as their very experience of self.

Unresolved traumas tend to stand out, creating a sense of separateness that can evoke deep discomfort.[29] If we identify with the trauma, we feel that we *are* this unease itself, perceiving ourselves as distinct and detached from the interconnectedness of existence. The resolution of trauma, however, grants us the freedom to release its grip, returning us to the effortless flow of peace. This can happen in many different ways, but rarely is it some ultimate pinnacle. Sometimes the release happens all at once in a moment of clarity, then out of habit, we return to our old thought patterns. It may be a slow burn, slowly releasing the grip over time until you realise, upon reflection, that you are living a much lighter life these days, having let go of something heavy and burdensome.

Whichever way it happens, it seems to me that what the human wants to do is let it go because peace, love and happiness is obscured while we cling to suffering. The 'inconvenience' of holding trauma is consistently felt as something holding you back in every day situations. If the pain of our trauma has no direct outlet, it absolutely will leak out in some other way. Repression, as a finite action, cannot endure forever.

Coping mechanisms can be used to assist with this weight, but it's clear that not all coping mechanisms are helpful. Remembering to breathe slowly and deeply when you feel stressed to stop you from hyperventilating for example, is a helpful coping mechanism. I'd say it's helpful because it doesn't involve denial of the circumstance but is simply a gentler way to ground yourself in the circumstance you find yourself in. It moves towards acceptance. Drinking alcohol or taking drugs in response to feeling trauma so that it can be ignored, forgotten,

---

[29] One could argue that this is especially the case for a social organism.

or repressed further would be more accurately described, as a *denial* mechanism.

Denial has negative connotations but it needn't be met with so much stigma, it's clearly a natural process, otherwise it wouldn't happen. When faced with an unsafe environment, whether it's mentally or physically threatening, denying or suppressing the presence of trauma becomes a way for the organism to continue to function in a way that allows escape from immediate danger. An unsafe mental environment may manifest as a relentless sense of self-criticism and judgment, while an unsafe physical environment can be characterised by aggression, forcefulness, or neglectful behaviours that disregard the well-being of others. In such circumstances, allowing the trauma to surface can trigger an overwhelming fear response, exacerbating the suffering.

Since vulnerability, in the form of open sensitivity, is always present but often shielded, it is plausible to consider denial as an expression of this very same profound fear response. Our own vulnerability, through conditioning, can come to be conflated with the threats we experienced *while* vulnerable. Denial then becomes a way to fight, flee, freeze, or appease in the face of our own vulnerability, seemingly for self-preservation. This process takes such a toll on our emotional and physical well-being due to the persistent internal conflict it generates. A fear of one's *own* feelings - the feelings that make up everything we believe ourselves to be: *self-*denial. This borders on saying, "I am not," the deepest absurdity.

But this cannot continue and it cannot last. Eventually, something has to give, and at that moment this conflict spills out into the physical world.

This trauma-release is seen as an active *recreation* of the traumatic event: the manipulation of an ordinary situation to turn it into one about the trauma. This willingness to tell the story of our trauma to the world and to ourselves is - in my view - an attempt to have it understood.

An issue arises when individuals who reenact their trauma fail to reflect upon their own actions, as this perpetuates their state of denial. Consequently, the internal struggle is repeatedly recreated and then externalised, fostering the belief that the world conspires against them, consistently presenting itself in the same hostile way. This reenactment unfolds with the intricate artistry of human communication, employing all available methods simultaneously. I call this phenomenon, 'The Human Performance.'

Performance And Reenactment

On the surface we could say that happiness is performed with a smile and maybe laughter, and we may perform sadness with upturned eyebrows and tears. But what the performance is really made of, is resonance. This resonance is the vibration pattern that we cannot make sense of when contextualised within the framework of the individual, the challenging notion that our inherent nature may not actually be unconditional peace and love but instead, turbulent chaos and fear. The Human Performance then, is an act of resonating at the frequency of that incongruence in attempts to communicate it to others. It is a reaching for understanding from others who may be able to help dissolve and release the pain of this schismatic sense of self.

When humans perform their trauma, they are recounting its narrative to others in the most immersive and intense way achievable by the human organism. It becomes a live-action role-play.

When we know someone very well and know their story, we can see what the roles are that have been allocated. For instance, sometimes the performer will play the traumatis*er* (perhaps a parent figure); sometimes they will play themselves as the traumatised, casting someone else in the role of traumatiser.

The following is a description of the trauma performance written from the perspective of someone who is aware of what they are doing. I feel this may be one of the best ways to explain it. From there, we'll go into example scenarios.

When I act as my traumatiser, this is demonstrating to you how I feel. It's not just an intellectual explanation of feeling so that you can feel sympathy for me, it is a live demonstration of the traumatic event where I act as my traumatiser, putting you in my shoes so that you might feel empathy as if you *were me*. By doing this, you will be able to understand the 'Me' I feel I am, and in this situation, 'Me' is the pain. It is the suffering that I am identifying with.

When I reverse the roles and instead act as the traumatised, that is, I feel the pain that I really struggle with, right in front of you, I am hoping you remember how it felt to be in my position and that your empathy continues through. I'm hoping that you show me you understand and show me that my feelings are not an obstacle, not a condition, to the presence of love. I am asking you, by nature of including you in my trauma through this performance, to help me see that the fear I feel is stopping me from feeling unconditional love, is not truly an obstacle.

I want to realise my unconditional love, peace and happiness in a place where I believed it was conditional. I want to demonstrate to you my pain so that when you have an understanding of it, you may be able to figure it out with me and help me understand it. You can help me let it go, quicker.

Now, a disclaimer: I won't play fair. When I perform I may switch from the traumatised to the traumatiser - from the aggressor, to the victim - or vice versa, at any moment. But what you need to remember is that it isn't a competition. It isn't that I'm trying to get the better of you - although it often does seem that way and I may actually say things that apparently have no other purpose. In truth though, it is really an attempt to reach out for cooperation. I am reenacting my struggles, my mental patterns, my physical tensions in a way that enables you to feel them too. Please, help me understand.

When I perform my trauma for you, it is not about you. It is so important to remember that, but it is initially one of the most difficult challenges you'll ever have to be awake to. The reason it's such a challenge is because I'll make it as applicable to the current situation as possible so that you become emotionally invested in learning about what is happening, precisely because it feels like it applies directly to *you*. Therefore, I'll make it seem as though it's *not* about my trauma and so unless you remember, you probably won't pick it up. That is again, another way that I don't play 'fair' so to speak, but if I told you what was happening, you're less likely to be invested emotionally and less likely to be able to help me figure out how to live with the emotional trauma.

Nevertheless sooner or later, as I remain in the role, I *will* say something that applies directly to the original trauma that may or may not fit with the situation. If you're aware of my trauma enough to see that, you may be able to realise this and switch towards compassion.

Even if you don't remember my trauma however, the argument will still provide an outlet to release some of the tension that has built up from the way my image of myself feels; so you're still helping in a way, though I appreciate how upsetting it is for you. However, if you could recognise my trauma before *I* do when I'm upset, by really listening to the whole performance I'm giving you - everything from my body language to my tone and verbal cues - and help me by remaining calm and showing me unconditional love by means of earnestly trying to understand me when I do this, you're doing me a service of the Gods.

You are returning me to myself when I feel most at odds with myself. When I perform my fears for you I am fearful and I am vulnerable. I want more than anything to be free of this fear. I want to rest once again in unconditional peace and love. I come to you to help me, to support me, and to understand me because I believe you can.

The performance comes in many shapes and forms. With practice, the trauma can be inferred from the performance without knowing the individual personally, based on the relationships they are demonstrating with those around them. There are many performances that are similar because they involve actions that demonstrate an extremely similar worldview. One of the keys to understanding performances of trauma, is knowing that children will often mimic their parents. Let's now go into some examples interpreted through this lens to help illustrate the point.

> 1. Boy X is feeling happy. He passes another boy Y. Y yells aggressively to X: "What are you smiling at? You think I'm funny or something?!" X senses and notices the aggression on Y's face and just keeps walking. Y yells again, "Where do you think you're going? Don't walk away from me!" Y grabs X and if X is unable to defend himself physically, he may get beaten up.

It seems to me that here, Y recognises himself in X in the form of happiness. It is possible that in this moment, Y is mimicking his home life - that when he looked and felt happy at home, he would get asked the same questions in the same aggressive way. Therefore, Y can be said to be performing his trauma for X. In this instance, Y is acting as the traumatiser, believing that X is capable of understanding him because Y recognises the innate similarities between them.

Y is certainly bullying X, but why? What if we view it differently, that Y is reaching out to X *in the only way he knows how*. This is how he has been taught to communicate. What does this tell us about the environment in which he is being raised? I contend that Y reaches out in an attempt to feel heard, understood, and loved.

It may be that Y is inaccurate, in that X cannot help him. For instance, if Y is looking for a way to stand up to his traumatiser, being confronted with the tremendous fear of X will not serve the purpose, and may just make Y feel worse - the last thing Y needs. If however X stands up to Y, it is likely that

Y will either attack, or, retreat. This interaction may then give Y the behavioural arsenal and impetus to stand up to his traumatiser that indirectly taught him these distressing beliefs in the first place.

Strangely there can be a sense of trust building if Y believes (on a deeper non-verbal level) that X is going to help him. If Y uses the strategies at home that X may have used in standing up to Y, and they fail, Y may come back to X with more aggression - as if Y trusted X to help and feels betrayed because X did not in fact help. Perhaps it was the case that mimicking X's behaviours at home even made it worse and the trauma is once again cycled back into the X and Y relationship.

Unless X and Y communicate (at first with the help of someone who has a broader perspective of these matters), and truly understand one another's entire environment - body, mind and surroundings - the conflict between them may continue indefinitely because each action towards one another would be reactive and taken out of ignorance.

The bully and the bullied have a chance to relate to one another and grow emotionally, to really learn something about the human condition. If X learned what Y's life was like, and Y saw that what is happening to him at home is not loving, the two could support one another very well. From my experience, it is also the case that victims of bullying *also* have troubled home lives, just in different ways. Where else would they have learned the resonance of victimhood? We can all learn something from everyone.

Let's look at another example.

2. In a romantic relationship, Alex asks if Sam would like to go to the beach. Sam snaps at Alex, "*We can't go to the beach it's too cold, don't be so silly*". Alex responds upset, "*I'm not silly I only asked you a question!*" Sam snaps back again, "*Oh calm down, fine we'll go if you're going to make such a big deal out of it*". Alex feels exasperated because now it's not fun anymore, it's a chore, and so bites back and raises their voice "*Why do you always treat me like shit?!*" Sam defends "*Stop yelling at me, you're always yelling at me!*"

In this scenario both Alex and Sam are using this argument to perform their traumas simultaneously. There is a lot of built up tension coming out and a lot of energy is colliding and creating friction, it gets quite heated quite quickly. It also means that with all the steam being let off, the truth becomes lost in the fog.

We could infer from Sam's response to the initial fun-orientated request, that Sam immediately jumps at the chance to perform their trauma for Alex. Sam assumes the role of their own traumatiser, embodying the character who would mock and belittle them for desiring enjoyable experiences. Alex is also struggling with a similar trauma and so all too readily engages in the role of the traumatised. Sam replies to Alex in turn with a response no one has ever been excited by receiving: reluctant agreement as if it was a favour, framed as if the other person was being irrational.

Naturally Alex is able to let more of their trauma out, as this may be exactly the type of situation they have found themselves in all too regularly. A lot of built up tension explodes out, swearing with exasperation. Sam however, switches roles from traumatiser to traumatised ("Stop yelling at me!"), perhaps with a new trauma triggered from the raised voice, or perhaps with the aim of both parties feeling understood from both angles. Either way, Sam changes the dynamic again.

From here Alex may switch into their traumatiser role and yell something like: "Why do you *make* me yell at you?!" or remain in the traumatised role: "You're being so mean to me!" This type of role switching is a form of 'gas-lighting,' though it isn't *necessarily* malicious. It is more likely down to chain reactions of The Story, reacting to past pain believed to be here in the present.

This is a vital note in understanding this concept here. The organisms are not merely acting as themselves; they are acting in accordance with their remembered pattern of vibrational sequence - *regardless* of who did or said what. This is demonstrated most clearly by the seamless switching of roles between traumatiser and traumatised. Recognise here that the energies present in a given interaction have us comprehending the world and ourselves in this way. Much like Skinner's pigeons, when feeling trapped, we frantically flap our wings and spin in circles, attempting to resonate in harmony with what we believe the world is, in the mistaken belief that this will maintain and lead to a greater sense of balance, order and peace. Therefore, interactions like the one between Sam and Alex can continue spiralling, even without any additional input from the other person as the domino effect of resonance chain remembrance is in motion.

Transcending The Role

Unless someone is able to break the chain of remembrance by finding some other resonance to align with, it will simply spiral until everyone is exhausted and nihilistic. Depending upon the chains of resonance, it could go in many different directions, from neglect to violence.

If we can insert a new resonance into our lives, it is extremely helpful to cultivate the resonance of being aware of, completely accept, and yet remain unattached to, our experience of mind. Practicing this in daily life can allow it to enter into confrontations and allow us to remain calm. This not only has practical benefits, but also physiological benefits as your system isn't flooded with cortisol quite so frequently.

It may become overwhelming at some point when attempting this during a confrontation. In that moment, if you cannot return to the accepting space - accepting even of your overwhelm - it's perfectly fine to ask for a break in the conversation. It could be as simple as, "I'm feeling overwhelmed and I'd like to give you and myself the loving attention we deserve but right now I can't do that. I just need to take a twenty minute break so I can recenter, and then I'd like to try to understand again." Take twenty minutes, then come back together at that time.

If they say no to the break but you can't stay without getting too overwhelmed and upset, then you can either explain again how you need to and are trying to take care of yourself and care for them as best you can; or, you can suggest taking it slower, one thing at a time. Or, as a last resort, you can simply say that you are going to take the break because there is no way you can continue without getting defensive (thus closing yourself off to both problem and solution).

Remaining unattached does not mean having no emotions; it means being fully aware of your emotions, feeling your emotions, but not losing sight of the fact that your pain is an experience within you, not the limits of you; it does not define you. Feeling overwhelmed often happens when we are given too much at once and aren't sure what to hold and what to drop, so we end up trying to hold too many things at once. We hold things when we take responsibility for them, and when we identify with them.

Let's imagine someone says, "You're an idiot". Do you take responsibility for that? Do you identify with it to some degree and are sensitive about it? Do you identify with the opposite of 'an idiot' and abhor the idea of being something other than what you think you are? Or, do you see that remark as a performance of someone else's trauma? Do you allow that anger and derision to stay with them, as *their* feelings expressed in this particular way? *Only* if we take what others give us and call it 'mine' do we get upset by it, because now we're holding it and identifying with it and we have to defend ourselves against its sting. Equally, when it feels as though someone describes something distressing and calls it 'you' or 'yours,' we can be led into defend the belief that it isn't 'me' or 'mine.' Just be mindful of this and apply the same principle. Allow it, accept it as a part of a performance of upset, and listen. Investigate with them.

If someone says, "You're an idiot" and we leave it alone, at the beginning the defensive reactions may still rise up within us. That's the hand that reaches for the object; it is the mental form of the taking-hand. That is merely a habit. Again, allow. Allow it to reach, don't punish it, you punish only yourself and that is unnecessary. But, notice that when you do not *become* the hand, and do not close the fist around the idea of being an idiot, the reach shortens. Watch your own reaching hand. After some time, long or short it depends upon focus and personal context, the hand will recede back to center and vanish. Seeing upsetting behaviour as their performance of their pain, and your upset as both your empathy for them and your performance of *your* pain, will significantly speed up this process. It will bring you rapidly around to compassion and in that, you allow yourself to radiate your true self: love.

Love has no identity that it needs to uphold. Identity dissolves in the face of love. When met with love, the identity of a past traumatised self cannot endure for long and is left with two choices: to leave and maintain itself, or to disintegrate right before your eyes, fading into the essence of its own dissolution. Love has the remarkable ability to transform and heal, gently unraveling the threads of past trauma and inviting the return of the ever-present and eternally liberated self.

Through a thorough knowledge of our particular mind patterns we can remain aware, accepting and unattached much more easily. Just as we don't get mad at the shape of a cloud, we don't get mad at the shape of our mind. We can show that same love and empathy toward ourselves at every moment. We can live from love rather than for it. We can abide in a resonance of compassion here and now within and as our very selves, rather than seeking it in the conditional behaviour of others.

The Monarch And Their Citizens

There are many metaphors for the mind that are intended to create distance between an observer and the mind, in attempts to stop the identification with its movements. One describes the mind as the trickster, a Gríma Wormtongue character, sitting at the side of a king (you) feeding false information, secretly ruling the kingdom. This has its merits, but it *can* appear as if 'the mind' is an actual agent - and a malicious one at that - trying to destroy the world. This has the potential to create opposition to this now internal villainous object called 'the mind' and so there rises an attempt to somehow stop it and fight it as if it were an enemy. The mind is NOT an enemy.

Instead, we can reframe the metaphor of the king and still give explanatory power to the nature of mind. We will use the term 'king,' though the character is just for the metaphor and the gender and sex of the monarch is ultimately irrelevant. Substitute it for queen if you prefer, but do try to look beyond it. The point isn't that a *man* rules the universe, but that there is a higher power beyond the fleeting experiences of the mind that give life to the mind.

So let's remain with self as the king, but instead, let's frame the mind as the citizenry. You sit on the throne in the great hall and, being the wisest one in the kingdom, the citizens come to you for help.

They enter into the great hall and are given the chance to share their pain with you. The way they do this is similar to the way bees dance for the hive. They perform it for you in a play. These performances are the memories and traumas of your kingdom.

The citizenry display what they have learned out in the world through memory, through repeating resonance of the past. The past event resonates in the present vibrating the way it did then, in hope that the wise king will understand and show them the way back to peace and love.

As the king, you're not supposed to get involved in the play. It's poor form as the monarch to cast yourself as a role and then start reacting to the characters being put on by the citizens. The monarch's job is to stay *out* of the play, to *listen* and hear what they're telling you about what is going on in your kingdom. Then, you are able follow them to where they want to take you. You may feel the play with all your soul and spirit, brought about by what you are being shown, but you must remember that this feeling is empathy for the citizens.

Through empathy, using the mirror neurones of the present, we can feel the pain of the past and reflect upon it. Feeling the pain doesn't mean believing we *are* the pain exclusively. If we do this, we lose the place from which we can be compassionate to the citizens as we risk entering into our own fear responses.

Sometimes the citizens can come to us with a story of great joy and we can laugh and have a wonderful time! We don't need to be cold and calculating to be an effective monarch. We don't need to shun emotion and lock ourselves away, far from it. The king is compassionate, and to be that he must be able to experience sadness, happiness, anger, serenity, depression, freedom, anxiety, and so on, but he must remember that he is not *in* the play, rather, the play is in *him.*

In the realm of the play, it is widely understood that the monarch does not exist as a separate entity, just as consciousness is not an object within the world. The king is not an extravagant figure adorned with opulence, transported in lavish carriages, and adorned with jewels. Instead, this king embodies humility and simplicity, recognising that he is not an individual to be worshipped above others. The king is inseparable from his kingdom. If the kingdom suffers, so does the king. If the kingdom is filled with peace and happiness, the king embodies peace and happiness. The king does not possess the citizens or the land; rather, his body reflects the state of the kingdom's well-being.

As the king strolls through the kingdom, radiating tranquility, the citizens are put at ease, and in return, their ease and calm are mirrored back to the king. It is a harmonious exchange, where the well-being of the king and the kingdom are intertwined.

The king's body serves as a reflection of the well-being of the citizens, but it does not limit the essence of the king. The true essence of the king is unconditional love, transcending the boundaries of any form. The body merely mirrors the perceived conditions of unconditional love within the local environment.

The embodiment of the king reflects the collective consciousness of the kingdom. The more conditions and attachments that exist within the kingdom, the more solidified and defined the physical form of the king becomes. On the other hand, when the kingdom experiences a greater sense of liberation and freedom from conditions, the king's form becomes more fluid and ethereal, symbolising a deeper connection to the boundless nature of unconditional love.

This king, when known in this way, opens the citizenry to healing. The king is not someone to fear. The king is open and loving. There are no likes and dislikes one must cater to. The king simply listens and understands the perspective presented by the performances. Over time, the citizens begin to realise that there is no need to be ashamed of their feelings because the king never shames them but only seeks to understand them. It is only within the citizens (thoughts) that shame arises. The king recognises that shaming the kingdom is self-defeating and counterproductive.

Royal Justice

When the citizens approach the king, seeking justice and retribution for their pain, the king does not respond with punishment or the establishment of laws. Such actions would be conditional, driven by control and reactivity, and would depart from the king's true nature.[30] The king's role is different. The king's action is consistent and unwavering: to dissolve the pain through love.

Love has no prescribed formula or set of rules. It is spontaneous and free-flowing, transcending the boundaries of conditional actions. While the citizenry may be consumed by anger and a desire for revenge, seeking to perpetuate the drama and pass on their pain, the king operates from a place of transcendent justice.

The king understands that true justice cannot be achieved by perpetuating the cycle of suffering. Instead, the king's approach is to dissolve the pain by offering love and understanding. The king embodies compassion, empathy, and forgiveness, seeking to bring healing and resolution to the kingdom. By responding with love, the king breaks the cycle of

---

[30] Reaction essentially meaning: to enact (a memory) again.

pain and guides the citizens toward a higher understanding and harmony.

The citizens, whether perceiving pain inflicted by their own thoughts or actions, or by others within or outside the kingdom, often seek to retaliate and return the pain they believe they have received. This cycle of suffering, an "eye for an eye" mentality, arises from the belief that they have been *given* pain and should respond in kind. However, the king recognises a profound truth: he is not *given* pain, but rather perceives pain, and it is up to him whether or not he internalises it as his own.

The king understands that these demands for justice are part of the performance, even if it seems like the play has ended. It is akin to breaking the fourth wall, where the king sees beyond the roles being played. He recognises that these demands stem from the belief that love is absent, otherwise the citizens would not have sought his intervention. By bringing their troubles to love and compassion, the citizens acknowledge them as the higher authority.

In this context, if the king were to consider their opinions and potentially act upon them for resolution, he would end up inflicting harm upon the world. Retaliation against either another kingdom or his own would only perpetuate a cycle of impoverishment in love and understanding.

The citizenry may say, "Let's take up torches and pitch forks and burn their village to the ground so they can know what it's like to mess with *us*!" To be reactive and loveless like this is one way to be a kingdom, but it's neglectful of both self and other, and ignorant of both the problem and the solution.

The king's ability to maintain a sense of detachment from the narrative of the performance is essential. If the king becomes attached to these narratives, he may inadvertently fuel them or attempt to appease the desires and demands that arise from them. This attachment can lead to a cycle of reactivity, where the king tries to prove the citizens wrong or succumbs to their wishes.

However, with a sense of detachment, the king is able to transcend personal biases and respond with clarity, wisdom, and vision. He can see beyond the immediate dramas and stories unfolding within the kingdom. This detachment grants him the capacity to perceive the far-reaching consequences of reactive actions, consequences that may elude the citizens in their moments of fury.

If the king spreads civil war in his kingdom through punishment, shame, ignorance and fear such as "I *shouldn't* think this" or "I'm so stupid" or "I'm horrible" or "I'm ugly" and so on, his kingdom will fall to fire and ruin and the memories that once defined it will be reduced to ashes. The kingdom/mind burns down and the king - unconditional love - will still be present, but is now will be surrounded by fear.[31]

So instead of reacting with violence, the king can engage the citizens in dialogue and ask questions to promote understanding. This approach dissolves ignorance and brings about enlightenment, fostering peace within the citizens themselves. By seeking understanding rather than resorting to violence, the king cultivates a harmonious society and avoids perpetuating a cycle of fear and vengeance. Destroying sources of pain through violence only perpetuates violence and fails to address the root causes of suffering. It creates a culture of fear

---

[31] Does this not sound like dementia? From this interpretation we can see that certain forms of dementia may well be linked to repressive/ abusive thought streams that create chronic fear and so chemically 'poison' the body. This may result in the reaction of the body to destroy (as a fear response) large parts of the brain like an immune reaction to a foreign body such as a virus.

and mistrust, whereas promoting understanding leads to long-term peace, and spiritual, emotional and intellectual growth.

The citizenry often perceive their suffering as unfair, feeling they don't deserve it. However, the king understands that actions and circumstances are not inherently fair, as fairness is a concept born out of fragmentation and ignorance. The king has the power to unveil the illusion of fairness. The king's true essence wants to permeate the entire kingdom with love and understanding, so that regardless of the events that unfold, there is a foundation of compassion and wisdom.

There are traditions amongst other kingdoms for the monarch to take on a specific role within the plays and performances of the citizenry: To be the 'ruler.' They have habituated themselves to becoming involved by means of control as if the monarchs had a specific idea of which performances should be allowed. "No, you must be *this* particular way," or, "I don't want to see another performance like *that* again!" In this, the essence of the king is veiled. The ultimate goal is lost upon the appearance of demands as love cannot be demanded. No one can *demand* that you love them. Love on command is not love.

Facing Fear

The monarch can become more at ease with their own citizenry as time passes; fully accepting that all performances are the best translations the citizens have, based on their experiences. For the king to judge the way in which the citizens perform their troubles is again an action of fear. This goes for the citizens in his own kingdom and those from another kingdom (someone else). In the moment of moral judgement the monarch puts an external conditional standard above his own, thus disempowering himself *and* his entire kingdom.

Perhaps there is the question: "How am I to act as the monarch of my own kingdom and not be ruled by fear?" Simply recognise that your loving nature is not a finite action that is done; your loving nature is the natural way of being and becomes more prominent after a shift in perspective has taken place. See that you, as pure presence, are not *in* any of the plays, any of the narratives that others tell themselves or that you tell yourself. There is no character that is entirely loving presence. Even if the play has a monarch in it with your exact physical description, that role is not you because you are not limited to a physical form. The physical form of the king is a reflection of the kingdom and the kingdom's influences (we may take this to mean genetics, environmental conditions, mind state and so on). You are the witnessing, pure Being beyond roles and limitations.

The task of the citizen is to display what happened. As the king, if you empathise with one character or another in the play so much that you then say, "I'm *in* this play" you begin to lose sight of yourself. The citizens want you to empathise because that is the only way you're able to understand the world from their point of view.

It may seem as though, if and when the king becomes a role, that he fails. But let's not frame it so bleakly. Getting involved in the play cannot be a failure; it's only the first part of the learning process.

The first part of learning is very often mirroring: "This is what it's like to be you."[32] At the beginning of the monarch's life they need to mirror like this. They need to *become* the citizenry so that they may fully understand them. The king

---

[32] As we see in the development of children. Hence, it matters more how you act around your children than what you say.

must become like them so that, in time, they may become like him.

If the king reacts by banishing the citizen from the great hall (repression), the pain is reluctantly cast aside from the king's attention. However, this approach is weakened by the literal guards of defence mechanisms, which are easily deceived by minor variations. Numerous specific defences and rules are put in place for situations that are unlikely to occur again, leading to complexity and overlap that hinders rather than helps. Here again see a parallel to Skinner's pigeons.

The citizen goes away with its pain still unresolved. It cannot let the pain go because the citizen is not apart from the pain but *is* the manifestation of the traumatic event. The king, by banishing the citizen (repressing the trauma), fragments his kingdom and so appears to fragment himself. The unresolved pain can only dissolve when met with the love and understanding found in the presence of the king's true self.

The banished pain will keep visiting the king wearing a different cloak each time and breezing past the guards.

The citizens, afraid of judgment and rejection, hide their true vulnerability behind a more recent issue. They fear approaching the king in their raw and exposed state, as they were once met with judgment, anger, and dismissal. Their vulnerability has become a source of fear, both for themselves and for the king. However, the underlying pain still resonates, seeking understanding and resolution through the similarities with the more recent issue, gradually gathering the pieces needed for healing. Gathering understanding this way however, may take lifetimes.

The citizen may never come back again as its own naked self, or, it may take a few minutes, a few hours, days maybe, months, years, or even decades. Often, the longer it waits the more likely it is that the king will be wiser and so more detached from the potential implications of the trauma that needs to be performed. This detachment will make the king more able to help the citizen.

Twenty years may pass and finally the citizen is able to pluck up the courage to return to the hall. The pain, manifest as a five year old, a ten year old, a sixteen year old, depending upon when the trauma occurred, stands in front of the king, still feeling the pain from decades earlier. The citizen says to the king, "It's me again, I'm still the same pain as I was - I have yet to find understanding. Can you help me?" And often, seeing a child in pain, whether someone else's child, our own child, or our inner child, will easily trigger love, understanding and compassion.

To prevent pain sitting for decades, the king could choose to leave the great hall and walk through the kingdom. This is a power of the king, to inquire into the nature of his kingdom, of himself; to be loving presence, offering it to all who come to see him.

To truly be himself, the king ceases to be anyone whatsoever. He sees that all ideas about who or what he is are ideas projected onto him by the citizens, and just because he is being projected onto, does not mean he *is* those ideas. He, really, is not even 'he'. Even ideas of what it means to be loving are left alone. It is not the love that is of objects, the love as opposed to hate. It's not the love of affection or a penchant. The king's true essence is beyond love, because the word 'love' is only a concept, but it is simply *called* transcendent love.

When ideas are left alone and are not identified with, there is a defenceless presence, and that presence is unilaterally a loving one that, in truth, needs no defence. It can never be injured; it has no form. 'The king' never existed as a separate entity and only ever took the form of that which reflected in unconditional love. 'The King' was more like a crowned mirror. And yet, we can look deeper.

A more profound insight shows that each citizen was, all along, the king. The thoughts themselves are only unconditional love, eternal being, formed in a way that either lets love flow, or resists love. The extent to which a thought seems 'malicious' is essentially the extent to which that thought resists the natural flow of love.

The Suffering Of The Monarch

If it is a struggle to see others performing their trauma for you, trying to be understood; if it's a struggle to meet them with this defenceless loving understanding, that's okay. Again, it can be overwhelming to be presented with stories of pain. Take an interval to ground yourself and detach from any role you may have assumed, and come back to loving presence. Try to see them as their own inner child, scared and alone, lost in the wilderness of fear, asking for help.

The rejections and judgements we have of our own kingdom (our own mind) and of other kingdoms are like wanted posters on the doors to the king's hall. Every rejection is an extra guard on the door and an extra stone on the wall. When we deeply open ourselves up we take down the posters, we lower the walls, and we remove the guards from their posts.

The start of this is as simple as sitting quietly and comfortably and offering love and understanding to any arising thoughts. Perhaps it is offered to sounds around you, to the sensations of the skin, to the breath, to the heartbeat, to the attention itself. The presence of 'The King of Heaven' is felt here in this defenceless giving of love.

If you want a deeper inquiry, we can ask where this King is sitting. Where is his throne? In other words, from where does this love emanate? Is it from the body? The body is loved, love does not come *from* the body alone, but saturates it. So, is there in fact any *specific* place at all? Or is it simply that your sense of presence itself is the ever-present love you seek, veiled only by the conditions and restrictions placed upon when to allow it?

Can you observe in yourself that the self-same dropping of the identification with defence mechanisms - the kingdom's walls, its citizens, its guards and weaponry (the 'Me,' the standards, the conditions, the judgements) - is what calls a halt to the illusion of conditional love? Can you see that unconditional love is ever-present in every interaction with the the citizens and others (mind & matter) and it is only through a belief in yourself as a specific character in a narrative that you begins to suffer?

The Story In Action

Human performance is the expression of the conditions we perceive as necessary for experiencing unconditional love. To foster a loving world, it is crucial to listen to ourselves and others with loving care and undivided attention. True listening goes beyond using only our ears and analytical mind to solve problems or showcase our intelligence. It involves listening with our hearts, practicing empathy, and seeking genuine understanding of others as they are in each present moment. By embodying this compassionate approach, we contribute to the creation of a loving world, benefiting both ourselves and those around us.

At times, a performance may be interrupted when a listener feels excluded because they haven't spoken about themselves for a while, be it minutes or seconds, depending on the individual. This feeling of exclusion often stems from insecurity, as the listener's self-importance is challenged when they prioritise simply listening to someone else. In the case of a fearful child, asserting oneself as essential becomes crucial for survival, particularly if it feels neglected. However, part of maturing involves transcending this need for constant external validation and permission, learning to nurture ourselves.

Now, let's consider the metaphor of the kingdom. As the monarch, imagine visiting another kingdom. Will you attend their court alone, representing the wisdom of your kingdom as a guest? Or will you bring your entire citizenry with you, potentially interrupting the performances of the other kingdom at any moment? You have been invited to observe, offer understanding, and share love, serving as a source of insight where the other monarch may struggle to see it.

You as the listener are vital. So just listen. If you are hit with, "Are you just going to sit there?" or "are you not going to say anything?" it's rarely not turned around with "I'm listening, this is clearly very important to you" or something similar, because it *is* very important to them and you *are* listening. We can, in this way, understand what people believe is of great consequence in their life - we can understand their conditions and perhaps, something about our own too. They are showing you something about life.

What usually ends up happening is that, while listening, perhaps reflecting back sometimes, summarising now and again, "Do you feel distressed when that happens?" or asking questions to clarify what you might not understand, you help the other monarch work the problem out for themselves. Your insights may be beneficial if they seek them, but ultimately, your words alone cannot teach them. They need the experience of going through it themselves and reaching a conclusion that creates a greater sense of understanding, compassion and wellbeing within them.

It's wonderful to be aware of the performance and the power we hold to change the world in an instant by dropping our identification with defences. It is, in my view at least, such a mesmerising beauty of life and allows a much deeper connection with others far, far beyond the superficial appearance of the physical. Humans, when performing their trauma, are looking for connection as they are asking to have their mind read and understood. And listening is, after all, the only way to read minds.

Mind Reading

When humans talk about reading someone's mind we often imagine it means hearing the verbal thoughts of others. Words are the last translation of any intention or vibration someone experiences and you will more often than not simply be told the verbal thoughts anyway, directly, indirectly, or sometimes sarcastically. The reading of a human mind involves understanding *all* languages of communication. The greater your knowledge and understanding, the more you can perceive and interpret the intricacies of the human mind. After all, if you see that mind and matter are not separate, how could this be denied?

If someone is having a menacing conversation in their head with themselves imagining it is you, they will act it out in subtle ways such as tone, emotional charge, body language, facial expressions and so on. All you need to do to read the mind is read/listen to the performance of the whole organism. This includes being open to context that may be informing their actions, context beyond what you may be aware of. Remembering this also helps us to stay unattached and yet compassionate and loving because we can accept and hold at the forefront of our minds that there are some things we do not know: "I can learn something from everyone". This is a more holistic listening. It's not listening to confirm what we *already* know (though it may do so), it's actively listening to potentially challenge and teach us things we may *not* know.

Any message we wish to communicate that requires tone, body language, facial expression and intensity to understand - something that is more open to interpretation - is already being communicated without words. For example, someone who comes up to you with a beaming smile, eye contact, arms wide, sounding very excited saying, "Well done," is a someone clearly very happy for you! The verbal congratulations are only confirmation of what you already observed.

By comparison, someone walks up to you slowly, arms folded, looking off to the side and occasionally glancing at you then rolling their eyes when they look back off to the side with an upturned mouth, and then saying sharply and sarcastically as they walk past you, "Well done" is very obviously NOT happy for you. Though they are trying - however unsuccessfully - to give the impression to others that they are by using the 'correct' words.

They *said* they were happy for you with verbal language, but with *every other* form of language, they said they weren't. Often words will be referred to after the fact as evidence of how they really felt, but, given the comparison above, it's perhaps more clear what's really going on. This denial appeal can also be seen as a performance.

This is the entry level of reading the mind of someone else. Beyond this it is possible to feel the emotions and needs of another as if they were your own, and beyond.

Knowing how to read all the other types of language, you can *infer* the words they were thinking that matched the other languages you were interpreting. These words you inferred may not be entirely accurate, but the same ballpark is very likely if you're a good read. Hearing the words from their mouth would have confirmed what you already suspected. Words are essentially confirmation; they are not the originator of intention. The *feeling* is first and the intellect translates it into verbal language later. So as Bruce Lee once said, "*Don't think! Feeeeel!*"

We can be conditioned to translate feelings into confusing or incongruent verbal language because words are secondary and so act as labels for what is primary. We can therefore mislabel feelings for example. However, the body *is* the feeling and so we can see feelings and emotions expressed more directly and congruently through a combination of observing tone, intonation, gestures, postures, and many other non-verbal cues.

Sometimes humans claim they didn't mean something the way it was received and that too *is* possible. It is always possible to misread non-verbal languages just like it is possible to misinterpret a sentence. It is also possible that we project our own feelings onto others and so read ourselves, via them. With experience you come to know the narratives and stories that you frequently project, and are able to differentiate that from when someone is performing their own emotional state. You can come to know when humans are attempting to defend themselves with their words and when they are being open.

Poles Of The Same Magnet

Humans, and in fact all living creatures, have senses that are all fundamentally senses dedicated to detecting vibration in various forms. The more varied the senses, the more comprehensive our perception becomes. Therefore, when we feel something and we resonate at that frequency, it can be detected by others. Of course, right? You've stepped into a room before and immediately recognised the vibe of it was a little off. You might have noticed that the resonance you detect when you enter a church is different to the resonance felt in a hospital, and those in turn are different to a forest. We *can* detect the resonance around us, and in us. Depending upon how you make sense of the places listed above, you will have different responses in your own resonance and relate to them differently.

So, let's say that since I was beaten up when I was younger, I have held the resonance of deep frustration. The story involves perceiving myself in the role of someone who is picked on, in the role of a victim. I may even have the experience that, "Those who pick on others seem to find me," and so come to believe that life isn't fair on me, further solidifying my perception of myself as a victim of circumstances.

But that isn't *quite* what's happening. As I abide in this narrative of myself, frustrated and put-upon, I am resonating at that frequency. I am therefore giving off the communication cues, perfectly detectable by others, that I am someone who can and will be picked on very easily because I already believe it is true.

Depending upon how we and others have been taught to respond to such vibrations, we or others will either avoid us or engage with us. The most likely one to engage would be someone who resolves the duality created within ourselves, that is, someone who acts as the counterpart to our one-sided story to create balance. In this case, that counterpart would be someone who 'picks on others'.

Now we have two humans coming together and using one another to exorcise their trauma. They say opposites attract, but opposites are simply poles of the same magnet: polar expressions of the same experience.

By living from the narrative of "I'm picked on," I recreate my life in the way that it has been, time and time again. I do however, simultaneously provide myself with the opportunity to transcend the narrative every time I reenact this story with another. I can take this opportunity to recognise the misery I am causing myself, then if I am intent on changing it, I can cease to hold onto this harmful idea that I am carrying around. I can do this by changing the story.

A good way to change the story is to create an intention to achieve something that you want only for yourself without telling anyone else about it until you've accomplished it. By doing this, you provide yourself with evidence that when you focus your mind and take determined action, you are capable of accomplishing anything you set your mind to. In addition, by eliminating the influence of external judgement, you gain insight into which judgements of yourself are actually originating from within you. Recognising these internal judgements allows you to consciously choose which thoughts to give weight and importance to, much like how you can choose whose advice or opinions you value and consider.

In the context of being targeted or bullied, there is a common phrase used to excuse the aggressor's actions: "They were asking for it!" However, upon closer examination, can we see that the dynamics between the individuals involved may have been operating on a non-verbal level through narrative resonance? It's not that the victim explicitly requested to be mistreated through their words of course; rather, between the two of them there was an alignment of energetic frequencies. One embodied the North pole (the aggressor) while the other embodied the South pole (the victim).

This insight has profound onward significance because it directly implies that the way children are raised is not about giving them rules to live by, but giving them roles to play. Raising children involves imparting narratives about the world and themselves, serving as frameworks for how they resonate and so how they interact with their surroundings. Our resonance, the way we vibrate energetically, defines our sense of identity, of who we are.

Looking laterally we see that the ancient Hindu traditions and the teachings of Sri Ramana Maharshi emphasised the fundamental question, "Who am I?" This inquiry directs our attention to the essence that exists prior to the narratives and constructs of identity that we create. It invites us to explore our true nature, beyond the transient roles we play in the external world. By submerging ourselves in this inquiry, we open up to the truth that precedes the emergence of the constructed self and in that, we find our inherent freedom.

It is better to understand oneself than to use force to attempt to overcome the events we encounter. For instance, it would not help me when feeling like a victim, to instead begin asserting my role as an aggressor. I am still defining myself as a victim, and using aggression and violence as a means to free myself - which will never work. My aggression is compensation for my fear. See this significant insight for its full context: This is true for all aggressors. A mere role reversal will not allow transcendence. Becoming the South pole rather than the North pole doesn't amount to much progress; magnets are after all, formations of atoms all spinning in the same direction. I am still in the same trap. This is, again, a point of view of separation and duality. It is an attempt to polarise life to my own advantage ultimately asserting the same worldview of persecutor and victim, dog eat dog, of competition, of *war*. Thus the world remains the same.

So be clear here. We actively *create* our environment depending upon the resonance we give out and the way in which we interpret and respond to resonance we receive. If we relentlessly observe the potential of something happening (an idea of the future, say) we give it ENERGY through focused attention and so we effectively give it MASS.[33] Therefore, it is bound to manifest as a physical reality. The more mass we give it, the greater its 'gravitational pull'. Here is the 'law of attraction' emerging one could argue. Mind and Matter, are not separate.

Unconditional

Some may contend that rather than love, it is hate, anger and conflict that are unconditional and it simply depends upon your

---

[33] $e = mc^2$

perspective. I'm open to discussion, but the experience is that we don't feel these things unconditionally. There is always an intellectual reason why anger, hate, fear and conflict are present, and it is always in terms of duality and separation. In other words, they are *inherently* conditional.

Again I reference sleep. If hate and conflict was the natural state, the unconditioned experience, we would not return from a deep, dreamless sleep feeling fresh, happy and peaceful; we would return *more* exhausted than before we went to sleep, having spent hours angry and fearful.

Everyone who's been in arguments where you've lost your temper will know that anger is exhausting. It's a dreadful waste of energy unless you're in a dangerous situation, in which case the excess adrenaline *could* be useful. But getting genuinely angry and aggressive over whether or not the towels were folded correctly is a telltale sign that something else is generating that anger. The towels are just an excuse to let it out.

You don't need the towels to be folded in that particular way, you need to be understood, you need to be listened to, and there are none better suited to that task than yourself. You understand yourself better than anyone ever could. Breathing deeply and slowly for a few minutes, taking a break to feel how your body feels and hear what it's saying will give a feeling of being understood. Do it now. Try it.

Listening to all of what you are, discovering the mystery of yourself, 'knowing thyself' leads to a quiet confidence and a gentle radiating peace. It's free; you don't need to subscribe for 9.99/month, you don't need a qualification or a professorship, you don't need equipment or a special building to do it in. Just listen, and have compassion for yourself.

Our attachment to conditions, along with our frustrated desire to be free of them, is an experience of suffering. When you next feel as though you are suffering, take a moment to look at yourself with your sense of knowing, not with your sense of sight, to see if this rings true. Are you trying to fulfil conditions so that you can allow yourself to relax into being simply what you already are? Have you put your inherent peace at the end of a journey strewn with obstacles? Do you realise that, even if the tools and materials were given to you by someone else, that the conditions you've set up right now, in this moment, are your own making? Who has the authority then, to dismantle those conditions to happiness? Are you willing to be happy and peaceful right now?

Trauma II

Unresolved trauma will often provide us with conditions to happiness, however small. In the case of severe trauma however, such as physical, emotional, mental, or sexual abuse, 'the world' is force-fed as a hateful and fearful place. These conditions seem much more challenging to overcome. Often the result is something like cPTSD, complex post-traumatic stress disorder.

The trauma is often something so unexpected or so shocking and fearful that without extended focused attention it will continue to re-traumatise us over and over again because we do not have the appropriate context in order to make sense of it. Often it results in nightmares of the event, and visual and physical flashbacks to accompany emotional flashbacks. Physical flashbacks aren't just a re-emergence of a memory while remaining aware of your surroundings, but almost like falling asleep and reliving the trauma in a dream, with the physical body re-enacting it. It can be heartbreaking to be a part of because the pain is so raw and what is exposed is so sensitive, but it is entirely *natural* of severe trauma - especially if it is repressed - and we needn't fear it.

There is so much to learn from the tremendous suffering that comes with severe trauma. Purposefully repressing anything like this will only cause it to leak out in other ways and it will continue to hurt us and others. It cannot be held down for our entire lives, it is too exhausting, too confusing, and it is altogether too much to ask of humanity.

By purposefully ignoring it or telling ourselves it is not okay to feel what needs to be felt, we are refusing to make sense of it. It can often be incredibly scary to make sense of what happened because it implies accepting it, and accepting that this immense fear really happened.

Importantly, the acceptance of our trauma can sometimes be conflated with saying it's acceptable - as if we now agree with it as if morally right. This is not acceptance. Acceptance is not denying any part of it. Acceptance is saying, yes, it happened, and being at peace with this fact. Acceptance is to no longer be at war with our memories, no longer resist them wishing they weren't our experience. Acceptance is knowing that they are the experience, and knowing that it's okay that they are the experience.

The trauma may be something you feel is wrong, but simply by virtue of experiencing it does not make *you* wrong. Your experience is what it is. What use is there in judging it and declaring it incorrect? There is no 'correct' way to exist. Your experience is what it is and has taught you about yourself. Any individual or culture (scale is inconsequential) that declares you broken or 'wrong' is simply ignorant and may well just be using denial to maintain that ignorant worldview based on their own fear and trauma.

There needn't be the stretch into self-judgement of what has been experienced; your own self-acceptance is more than enough to free you.

Using Time

We are able, through the simple ubiquitous power of awareness, to give our conditions Time - to give them the spotlight in experience. When they are on stage, they perform for us. They tell us terrifying stories and wonderful stories. But when we see the whole act through, when we keep listening and giving space infused with love, they begin to loose their power. They can no longer shock us as they used to because the more we listen, the more we know their ins and outs. We're not left creating even scarier beginnings or endings in our imagination. From this moment on, the performed condition begins to decay and dissolve into the sands of Time.

The memory of it will likely remain in some form because it is - whether we like it or not - a monument to the ability to learn and transcend the fleeting nature of appearances. It is an understanding gained. Nevertheless, the power it has over us can be reduced to zero and although we *can* remember it, we are no longer thinking about it on any kind of frequent basis. This is not because we are repressing it, but because we understand and accept it. It was a means to protect ourselves and make sense of ourselves when we did not understand. We begin to stop looking to our conditions to inform us about who we are and how we would like to be.

It can certainly be helpful to have someone else with you when you expose your trauma to the spotlight of your attention; it could be a therapist, a family member, a partner or a friend; someone there to hold your hand when you 'visit the underworld,' to be your lifeline if it gets too much. Similar to Pandora's box, once we confront our trauma, there is no turning back to our previous state; we've eaten the fruit of knowledge in the garden of Eden. Knowledge clues us in to our previous ignorance and from here we have two choices: we can either repress and torture ourselves, or open up to deep compassion and full acceptance of our experiences.

Remember that the fearful self is an experience we are aware *of;* it is not the fearful self that is aware. There may be the feeling of dying and succumbing, but that feeling is worth understanding. Hold steady in your loving presence. Accept that these feelings, these sensations and perceptions are manifestations of *you.* You are the totality, modulating as these experiences. There is no right or wrong, there is only what is. Do you accept it?

We can have a very deep sense of empathy for our experience from here. We can feel sorry for ourselves, cry for ourselves, understand ourselves and show unconditional love from this space, *as* this space, completely without judgement. We can envelop our fear in unconditional love rather than feeling like we are enveloped by fear. We can be at peace in the *acceptance* of the visceral experience of such terrific sadness and despair. It is neither bad nor detestable, nor is it weak to be sad, it is a TREMENDOUS strength, a godlike strength, to accept the sadness of suffering. After all, if a god were incapable of feeling sadness and despair, what kind of limited and conditionally loving god is that?

In the true acceptance of suffering there is a death and a rebirth.

There is inescapable beauty in the destruction of what we're clinging to as we learn to let go of our attachments to suffering and who we thought we were. Likewise, if we are attached to the idea that we must ALWAYS be joyful and excited in order to be 'well balanced' or considered happy, we are still suffering the same fate. Happiness is also visible in the peace and love present in the acceptance of whatever comes our way - simply enjoying the nature of Being.

Sadness is an opportunity to learn about humanity, about the vast complexity of life. There is a deep wisdom in sadness and we would be remiss to ignore it.

Men & Mental Health

I would like to take this opportunity to address something that is rearing its head out of taboo, and that is the mental health of men. There is a lot of pain and suffering trapped inside men. Being sent off to war, most recently throughout the twentieth century, caused immense trauma across the entire world.

We see in more modern times that a large amount of soldiers are often diagnosed with post-traumatic stress disorder (PTSD). Of course, it isn't that this is a new phenomenon; it's that now the effects of war on humans are better understood by western psychology as a particular field of study. They were deeply understood in Ancient Japan, seen in the traditions of the Samurai.

However, when those with trauma - be it from war or otherwise - are given no help to understand what happened to them and are just expected to immediately 'return to normal' (a uniquely manipulative phrase implying knowledge doesn't change us), all we end up with is repression and the trauma leaking out in destructive ways.

These destructive ways are not faults of the individual, but again, a performance of what it feels like to experience life from that point of view. The films Rambo and The Hurt Locker were important for many reasons but especially because they spoke to this very issue. Men have been expected to repress sadness and despair and 'do their duty'. To 'be a man' can then translate as: 'to repress emotions'. This is ostensibly very practical in a traumatic situation to aid getting out of it alive, but due to the extended period that war goes on for, it isn't just one battle and then ample processing time once the battle is over. War is not definable as: dealing with an immediate threat once and being free of it. War is extended conflict - be it in the home or on the battlefield. War goes on for *months* and *years* at a time, which means repression is no longer a temporary fix, but may become habitual.

From here the bigger challenge is to break this habit and allow oneself to experience *years* of trauma, while at the same time not surrendering to the old ways of dealing with trauma by repressing it.

Societies or countries bent on war are not those sensitive enough to wellbeing to provide this kind of time for healing. So what happens? The trauma can very easily be passed on to children, to family, and to friends. It is performed for everyone because war is such a confusing and conflicting event, being so inescapably harmful and loveless for everyone involved.

The outlook for this performance is perhaps described accurately as: if anyone can understand - even if only a little - it will be worth being vulnerable again in order to let go of some of this pain. See that war is extended conflict, and if we breed internal conflict by denying what is natural to us, we are living life at war with ourselves.

Implication Of Responsibility

Those who appear to need compassionate attention don't know how to give it to themselves in that situation because the prevalent culture does not teach children how to. Capitalist culture at least, grows by feeding on telling the population they're sick in order to sell them the cure. Reacting to someone in need or in pain with judgement and derision would not only add to their trauma cycle, but would be a denial of your own in the face of pain. When you are in need or in pain, what is the most likely response you'll offer if you train yourself to judge pain and needs in others?

So we just have to ask ourselves which direction we want to steer the ship of humanity. Do we want to steer it towards trauma and isolation, or towards compassion and oneness?

In many instances of trauma, conflicting beliefs arise to perpetuate it, to hold the course to trauma and isolation. For example, in the context of war, the expectation to 'be tough' or 'stay strong' (suppressing sadness) and the expectation to kill other beings work hand in hand. If you feel devastated when you kill someone, you can't and won't *keep* killing, and that's bad for the war business. The narrative of 'toughness' and justifying the act of killing by telling stories about its merits serves as a conditioning that desensitises the population to violence. Note how soldiers - irrespective of the nature of their conflict - are often branded as heroes. Defending one's own country within its borders is one thing, but invading a different country and attacking its people is another, is it not?[34]

We find many children after the war that were beaten by their parents (and teachers) and *also* taught to repress the pain. The trauma is diluted in a small way i.e. no killing, but a large part of it - the mental attitude - is clearly passed on to the next generation.

I believe it makes sense to say that trauma releases via performance so that it dilutes itself by dissipating throughout the social group, allowing the opportunity to raise the

---

[34] You can defend your house from an intruder, but if I went to someone else's house to take their things and claimed to be defending myself from them, how long would that defence stand up to peer review I wonder.

collective understanding of the entire group all through one individual's experience.[35]

Without being aware of this, we may create narratives seen in the understanding of the middle ages. That of these traumatised individuals being 'possessed'. Strangely though, if we don't take it literally but metaphorically, it makes sense to get a priest to 'exorcise the demons', if and only *if* the priest was simply offering the 'Unconditional Love of God'. Unconditional love is an extraordinarily helpful course of action in the recovery from trauma as it includes listening and understanding - not preaching or commanding. However, as many will be aware, it likely wasn't about a priest coming over to listen gently and lovingly.[36]

If we are unaware that trauma can be inherited from others, it makes it much more difficult to understand what's going on. We can get caught up in the performance and take on someone else's trauma as if it were our *fault* or problem. Circling back around to the mental health of men, if men are picking up the idea that to cry or show sadness or distress is weakness and weakness is to be avoided, it doesn't stop them feeling it, it just stops them expressing it in a healthy way. The repression is self-destructive, and then surprise surprise, we see a huge amount of outward aggression as a rebellion against this impossible standard, and then waves of depression. Taking this

---

[35] The entire group could be humanity as a whole, or even all of life.

[36] Arguably, and slightly as a side, the action of commanding the demons to leave the 'possessed person' demonstrates a departure from Love (of God) as the truth and heart of the priesthood, and a movement towards Fear (of God) taking its place. A gentle slope towards blind conditioning. This is a danger of obedience to dogma, be it religious or in any other setting. When the point of doing something is lost it degrades into mechanical and impotent tradition.

into consideration, it's no wonder that we see suicide as a leading cause of death in men.

This isn't limited to men of course. A world culture that is repressive and denial-centred is detrimental to almost every living being on Earth, setting standards of behaviour from a standpoint of ignorance. Women are not forgotten by any means, they have also been forced to repress their feelings - especially feelings seen as more energetically masculine such as anger. In actuality, this separate and dichotomous worldview is dividing everyone from each other, and also, within ourselves.

What is humanity doing? Why are humans so keen to limit and contort themselves?

Humans aren't either feminine beings or masculine beings, humans are feminine-masculine beings and masculine-feminine beings. These are energies of behaviour, not genitalia. There's no sense in trying to get humans with male genitals to align with only masculine traits any more than there's sense in trying to get every magnet with a north pole to be only the North pole. Males and females can be both gentle and aggressive, but gender and sex have nothing to do with it unless we insist upon contorting the psyche to repress half of itself.

The enormous explosion of gender identity in the psyche of humanity demonstrates this all very clearly. Life cannot be confined to these absurd boxes of arbitrary behaviours. The terms 'woman' and 'man' extend far beyond mere biology. Those terms imply behaviours, expectation, they imply a frame of mind, they imply a 'socially appropriate' sense of self, they define *for* us an identity crafted by another. This outlook is divisive, repressive, depressive, and ultimately a denial of what humanity really is: absolutely complete as a natural expression of the totality of Being.

A rebellion against the dichotomy of 'man or woman' is a rebellion against a divisive reality. Again, as we develop, we make some thought patterns stronger than others. The more Time we invest in thinking certain things or acting in certain ways, believing certain beliefs and so on, the more solid it seems to become. The more concrete it feels, the more mass it seems to gather and so the bigger its gravity, meaning more thoughts are translated through - and seen relative to - this now massive concept of self.

Based on this logic, it seems important then to say that dividing ourselves into even smaller categories of gender or sexuality is something that only creates more boxes by which to isolate ourselves and it won't remain if we are to have true progress towards a lack of repression. Sooner or later, we will tire of *those* boxes. The freedom is not in having your own unique box, that's prison. The freedom is getting out of the mindset of boxes altogether.

If we truly want to transcend, we have to stop looking for a solution with the same thinking that created the problem in the first place. We can't use division to see the whole. This goes for the psyche and for the field of physics. We have to stop isolating ourselves from yet more people by defining ourselves even more rigidly. Humans seem to get upset about someone being or saying they're different because it makes them insecure about who they feel *they* are. It's just fear, and they're performing their fear by means of an attack against someone else. It's a fight response. There is no benefit to either party in making someone else's trauma and fear *your* enemy.

Can we try instead to educate each other lovingly when there is a disagreement? If the other is unwilling to stop being violent, the bravest thing is just to walk away in love. Why use the punishment (to both parties) of violence to try to stop behaviours we dislike in others? - Behaviours we perceive as violent. Doesn't that just keep the cycle going on a more fundamental level? Violence in the name of peace is nonsense...

Perceiving The Performance

When we understand as human beings, it very frequently involves relating some of what we're learning to our own previous experience. We can imagine that it was *us* feeling the pain that is being expressed and we can begin to help others profoundly. Here, we understand them *as ourselves*, not as something *other* than ourselves.

The performance is the single most powerful way a human communicates. It goes way beyond the dripping tap of words alone and collapses the entire dam using all possible communication methods at once. The performance is a turning inside out of the ordinary human experience where the internal psychological experience is laid bare in a brave and open external physical expression.

To be performed to is something of a privilege, as in many ways it is a cry for help to *you* directly. I repeat: the performance will be made more specific to the situation at hand because it is an attempt to get *you* emotionally invested in the narrative. When you are emotionally invested, the potential for empathy of any given human being is significantly higher, but it does carry a risk of rejection. Nevertheless, empathy is the goal of the performance, not sympathy. Sympathy is like pity and is not the same as understanding. True understanding is transcendence, pity is just confirmation.

When the curtain goes up on the performance, if we are attached to our personal identity it is much more likely that we will defend this identity in the face of what is perceived to be a direct attack on our personhood. If we travel the world like this, every performance simply becomes an argument, a conflict, judgement, and then isolation from each other and everything else. We become *things*. Again I say ad nausium, the goal of the performance is to be understood! To dissolve the personhood! We cannot be empathetic in opposition to one another, yet the paradox here is that the performance seems to be *creating* opposition: Me vs. You.

I've become more and more convinced over time that coming into a paradox is a sign of truth - especially when it comes to unity because it shows there is something inseparable about the two phenomena. The truth I think we can derive from this, is that trauma itself relates to the notion of separation and conflict.

Conflicts can end with one side obliterating the other - providing a facade of peace. We saw this with South West Asia ('the middle East'). 'Western' countries went there to try to destroy 'the opposition,' but this only resulted in a retaliation and militant 'rebels' reenacting the trauma inflicted upon them. Oblivion is impossible and is no way to bring about any true or lasting peace; this is using fire to destroy fire.

Let's say it was me who was performing. If you shout me down I may either try to burn more intensely than you and it gets heated and may become physically violent; or, like a star under pressure, I may begin to collapse under the emotional weight of repressing my trauma. So the importance of listening is paramount.

If we went to the cinema, what is our response when during the film one of the characters gets very upset and yells aggressively at another character? We listen, see it from their point of view and feel empathy for one character or the other. We may subtly identify with one of them, as their story is similar to ours. But what if instead of doing this, we got personally insulted by what the character said, stood up, yelled at the screen, and walked out? "Don't you talk to *me* like that Ryan!" It's ridiculous! A film is trying to communicate something to the audience: *feeling*. In like manner you are the audience for the performance of trauma - the attempt to communicate feeling.

If we weren't performing in order to communicate feeling and be understood by one another, why would humanity turn performance into an entire school of art? Skilfully performing emotional states and psychological messages is what acting is. That's why the very best actors don't just speak the lines, they PERFORM the lines and just happen to speak the words at the same time.

So being able to recognise and read the performance is the first step. The second is to be a good audience member. You don't yell out in the middle of a play, "Oh I see, this is a performance! I thought you were *actually* mad at me!" You destroy the communication that way and the very real expression of emotional distress is trivialised. The genuine desperate attempt to feel understood so that someone can understand their trauma and feel free of its believed conditional restraints upon unconditional love would then seem like a joke, as if it's being forced and it really isn't genuine. It is genuine, and calling attention to it *can* just come across as invalidating.

Invalidation of it by calling attention to it is of course context dependent. If two people understand the metaphor and see its validity as a tool of comprehension, it can be a way to 'find the way home' by calling attention to it in a loving way. In that context, bringing the performance to the awareness of the other might be extremely helpful. Ultimately I'm calling it a performance to make conceptual sense of it, but at its core, it is communication of the deepest insecurities and fears humans have. The goal is simply to find a way to acknowledge that, and love each other.

When we want to feel understood for something that's upsetting us, the last thing we need is for someone else to take some supposed moral high ground and trivialise our upset.

That's not understanding and nor is it compassion, it's just more insecurity masked in superiority, and from the perspective of sadness, the mask of superiority is not as opaque as it looks from the point of view of the one holding it. Someone in the throws of a performance can often see right through the games of the ego.

An understanding of the performance of trauma isn't an excuse to feel superior. The recognition of the performance of trauma is the surface layer; it is the first step because recognising it is only the invitation to a deeper more profound understanding of another human as yourself. Conceptualising it as a performance is a metaphorical signal, a reminder, to allow you to see opportunities in which you can allow yourself to be compassionate and feel less inclined to defend yourself. It is your natural way; just don't listen to the line of thought telling you to repress the truth of who you are as a loving being.

Like in the story of Buddha, it can be *us* who in the face of the angry man who yelled and spat, met him with love. Meeting the angry man with love, with compassion, the anger reflects back on him and he is inescapably found in a state of self-reflection.

We must - figuratively - sit on the floor with each other. Assume no moral high ground over one another, erect no pedestal for ourselves, and take not the spotlight for fear of seeming irrelevant. The performance of trauma is an assuming of stage presence in the story of a tragedy and as the audience (or the opposition) you are vital.

Every tragedy has sadness at its core. Once both the performer and the 'audience member' genuinely hit that place of sadness via vulnerability and empathy, there is an opportunity for understanding, there is true communication; there is *communion*.

It seems obvious to say that a tragedy is sad, but the performance often begins with aggression and anger (defence of the vulnerability) so it is not always immediately obvious. This is why it's very easy to get drawn into the role you're given by the performer who wants you to be involved. Nevertheless, if we are listening from the place of love, we can see the role we are being given and we can be the 'mole' in the play. We don't have to actively refuse the role, but we *can* simply not perform the role and be loving instead. Watch the performance and *feel* what is happening. Too much emphasis is put on logically *analysing* life. This is neither the limits nor the most powerful aspect of being human. The combination of emotional intelligence and intellectual intelligence is infinitely more powerful than either on their own. A seed here and a flower bed over there is potential; but combining the seed and the flower bed creates something magnificent that is both and neither all at once - it can just take time for us to be aware of its fruits.

In many ways it's a risk to listen so openly and empathetically because we are making ourselves more vulnerable to what appears to be a threat. We are opening ourselves up to the world and to others by allowing them to affect us, but this is the most magical thing because in this we reveal to ourselves that we *are* the world. Everyone and everything, is us. When we are affected by the world in this way we are not beaten up by the world, we are not attacked by the world, we are not destroyed by the world; we are enlightened by the world. The world teaches us about *ourself*, we know the world more intimately than any sexual experience could show; we know ourself as a profoundly deep and all-pervading Unconditional Love.

Be that loving presence for others and yourself. Listen to yourself; allow yourself the experience and rebellion against a conditional love. Know that you *are* good enough. You are love itself. After all, when you love another, where else does your love come from but you?

10

God

KEY PRINCIPLES:
BEING & INFINITY

Infinite God

How does the notion of 'God' fit into this? The Abrahamic God is said to be limitless by followers of that tradition. God is the eternal and infinite Absolute. The Qur'an says in chapter 112 verses 1-4, *'Allah is one, Allah the Eternal, begot no one, nor begotten. Nothing, is comparable to Allah.'* Is this not exactly the same as Infinite Being? In the book of Elijah, The Old Testament refers to the *"Everlasting God."*

In other traditions such as Buddhism, in The Diamond Sutra for example, Buddha says, *"If infinitely many galaxies actually existed, their only reality would be in their cosmic unity. Whether as microscopic powder or as galaxies, it makes no difference. Only in the sense of the cosmic unity of ultimate being can the Buddha rightfully refer to it."* The Yoga Vasistha talks of *"Brahman the Infinite,"* and at the beginning of the Dao Te Ching it says, *"The Dao that can be spoken is not the eternal Dao..."*

So I ask, in this limitless and infinite-ness to which almost all religions refer, where is the space for a separate and *independently existing* individual? Where is the space for the separate worshipper? Jesus answers that there is no distinction! "*I and the Father are one.*" Buddha answers in the Diamond Sutra that there is no distinction! "*In truth, there are no teachings and there are no Buddhas.*"

Where even, is there a space for a mighty ruler as an individual, a separate being that judges and hands out punishments and rewards accordingly? These are finite and conceptual notions. These are, in religious language, idolatry. To worship a notion, a concept, a limited god, is to worship an idol, isn't it? As the story of Moses seems to be pointing to, no matter how elaborate the idol - made of rare metals, in a form representing divinity and prosperity as an agricultural society (the golden calf) - it is nevertheless *not* 'God'.

So the way in which I have come to understand the term God is a meaning equalling the same as the term Being.

To worship a finite concept as a deity is symbolic, representative of aspects of infinity such as wealth, sadness, pleasure, intoxication, pain, anger and so on. Similar to the way Ancient Greek traditions are viewed from the present time. Atheism became somewhat of a movement over the past few decades, but in the process has also characterised God almost exclusively as a deity of judgement. There are undoubtedly many people who act as if this is the case. Many crimes against humanity, against peace and love, have been committed in the name of judgement and a sense of moral rectitude. This has occurred all over the globe from many different religions for many generations. But don't be fooled, behavioural judgement and political order are finite affairs of the mind, and not, in the grand scheme of things, what 'God' is really about.

Judgement sets an arbitrary limit on the extent to God and God's love.

The organisations that form in an attempt to defend and protect God, invariably fail. Their defence involves the necessary restriction of infinity and so the creation of a finite idol. Then the idol is protected, not God.

In truth, God needs no defence. If God is truly believed to be infinite, God must be everything that is, all at once. God must be everyone and everything possible. If God is infinite, God is the totality. There cannot be, in a belief in infinite God, any room for a true separation between an individual worshipper and 'Godself'. There can *only* be God. God is the homeless woman on the street and the billionaire on the yacht. God is the trees of the forest and the insects that live inside them. God is the human and the Earth, the stars and the galaxies. God is, without exception. Always.

Not even *you* can be separate from God.

God, Buddha, Tao, Being. These are not personal entities with which you have a relationship of one to the other; they are the impersonal totality, both the context and content of relationship itself. They are simply different words for the same thing: Conscious Infinite Being.

In the realisation of this, the 'belief' in God transcends into the living experience of the self *as* God. That self you feel yourself to be, is the same in and as, everyone and everything.

The Love of God

How can we speak of God's love? Is it the fear-based concept of love? A love given to you from outside upon performance of the correct conditions, rituals and rights? Does one 'deserve' the love of God through conditional action, or is it otherwise?

Deserving something is a concept rooted in the belief of justice based on specific actions. This belief can lead to idolatry, which perceives God as a limited, finite being with supernatural abilities. According to this belief, love is seen as a reward bestowed upon individuals based on their 'right' actions, while fear and pain are viewed as punishments for 'wrong' actions - the standards of which are decided by the people. This perspective also extends to the notion that natural disasters are divine retribution for perceived wrongdoing.

But let's stop for a second here. The limitations on this god are numerous. This god is limited by some moral standard that seems to come from outside itself because this god seems unable to change it. Does God's moral standard come from outside God? That shows a limit to God, a boundary where the morality of God lies, and where God sits - and so this *cannot* be God if we are to see God as infinite.

God's moral standard must come from the nature of God itself. So, is God's nature loving? If the answer is no, "Why are you worshipping pain and suffering?" is perhaps a better question to explore. If the answer is yes (whether taken on faith or not) that must come with the corollary that since God is infinite, God's love must be infinite. If God's love is infinite, love must be infinite and must be within everyone. The love of God must be present in every single experience that is ever known, though it may be ignored or veiled by conditional belief.

If we decide that there are certain people, certain living beings, that do not 'deserve' God's love, we are operating under the belief in a limited and finite god, one whose love is conditional and limited. If we are ever to truly believe in an infinite all-loving God, that love cannot be conditional.

I'd like to venture a hypothesis that God's love was portrayed as something attainable through right actions for a specific purpose. It is observed that individuals who engage in harmful behaviour often experience suffering, which may create a sense of justice that they are not deserving of love as a consequence of their actions. Murder, for instance, cannot be condoned through the experience of God's love.

What if we switch this around? What if we say those who feel they are in the absence of God's love/God (which is simply love itself), are naturally in the presence of suffering. This perceived absence of love *is* the suffering and the suffering is the reason for the terrible action. Then, naturally, harmful actions are the spread of the perception of the absence of love and so, the spread of suffering.

So what if love is not a consequence of right action, not an effect of a cause, not a *reward*, but is the reason for what we *call* right action, is the cause of the effect of right action. What if it is the start-point upon which the concepts of reward and punishment are based?

If the veil of ignorance is drawn over the mind it might lead one to believe that they are separate from God and so they do not feel this unconditional infinite loving presence. In this, they act to deserve it, to attain it through satisfaction of conditions. If there is a thick veil, potentially given by means of strong narratives of unworthiness such as 'being born a sinner,' there may come a belief that they are someone who is *never* deserving of love and may abandon the quest to discover love.

But obeying the commandments say, is not really, when viewed in this way at least, ever about deserving something that is not yet given but will be later. Obeying the commandments could be viewed simply as a starting point to feel the love of God *here and now*. If God is infinite, and the nature of God is love, then the infinite love of God cannot be absent at any moment. It must *always* be present. So, it is present *now*. Why push only for reward in an afterlife? Why can infinite God's infinite love not be present now? It isn't a question of mechanism; it is a question of whether or not there is a belief in *a* finite god or *infinite* God.

Finite gods would have limited powers both in space and time. Is that the God that is being worshipped or represented? If so, there is something *greater* than this god and that is labelled as Conscious-Infinite-Being. If God is infinite, then it is truly unlimited in every way.

The love of God is not given upon death as a reward for a good life; the love of God is ever-present as God is. The only reason anyone may not feel this omnipresent love is due to a belief that it is not present and is instead contained within and originates from *some* finite experience.

How, you may ask, could the belief of a tiny insignificant human defy the nature of God if God is so infinite? Again, if this is asked, the point has not sunk in. There are no actual tiny insignificant humans that defy some separate God. God is the all. The play of being an insignificant human *is a play of God.*

You ARE *God.* Certainly not that the individual 'Me' is God, implying other things are not; rather that God plays the play of being an individual. God is the ocean and the 'you' or 'me' is the wave.

The wave is not the nature, the foundation, of the ocean; the ocean is the nature and foundation of the wave. You are not the foundation of God, but God is the foundation of you.

What that means is that the waving that is this finite self, running around the place trying to act correctly and deserve love, is, by doing so, only acting to postpone the experience of the love it is hoping to find. By realising the nature of one's true self, by self-realisation, this transcendent love is known as the very nature of Being itself; and the entirety of all that is, is seen to be saturated with it.

The Three 'O's.

OMNISCIENT	OMNIPRESENT	OMNIPOTENT
All Knowing	Ever-Present	All Powerful

If we ascribe these as attributes or 'abilities' of a god character, things become murky very quickly. We end up falling into terrifically deep pitfalls around questions of morality. Pitfalls such as, *"If God is all-knowing, He knows everything that is happening. If He is all-powerful He has the power to change things. Why then, when God knows of suffering, does He not change it? Does this not prove that God is not loving?"*

Of course, this is a wonderful counter-point and its very difficult to defend against. To try to defend this would simply be to invent an answer based on your own limited concepts - as if an all-knowing, ever-present, all-powerful god would need the help of a limited human mind. This god would be hearing the question, be present in the room, and still choose not to answer even though it had the power to do so.

This puts the finite god hypothesis into deeper trouble when the notion of eternal reward and eternal punishment are added to the actions of every human. A finite god that is able to remove doubts of his reality and so save people from eternal punishment, but doesn't, is an act of evil that even the limited human mind can see is nigh-on unforgivable. To punish ignorance, an ignorance created by what can only be assumed as a purposeful lack of education, and on top of that determine to *never* forgive is... absurd.

This position is, thankfully, *not* what is defended when *most* religious people talk of God.

How then can these three O's be made sense of if they are not traits of a limit being?

Lets take omnipresence first. Is infinity always present? We have already established many times before that it is. If there were a limit to its presence it would be finitude. Therefore, even the questioner who doubts the validity of the argument of a finite god's omnipresence is God. 'The All' is God and God is 'The All'.

What of omnipotence? What does it mean to be all-powerful? Again, we can't, if we are being at all consistent, imagine this to be like a superpower of some sort. As if a big dude with a beard sitting on a heavenly throne (like a modern Zeus character) has the power to do anything it wants. It cannot be a trait of a finite entity. Infinity is not an *object* of worship or reverence. Any such reverence would only be infinity finding reverence for itself and the experience of reverence would be its own self, feeling the reverence contained within itself. The 'power' is not a power of control *over* other objects separate from God. God is all there is, so it is therefore the word 'all' that must be reframed.

It is perhaps not that *a* god has 'all possible powers' as in, has accumulated or is in possession of *every* possible finite power or ability: to turn your hair green, or make the world shrink by a factor of ten, or make a rock so heavy god couldn't lift it. It is perhaps more accurately viewed as every action that *is* done, is done by the only reality that is - which is what the word God refers to, the only reality that is. So when reading 'omnipotent' it may in fact be better to read that as, 'there is nothing that is done, that is not done by God because there is nothing *other than* God'. All powers, or perhaps, all action, is the movement of God.

We can also draw a parallel to Quantum Mind Hypothesis in that, depending upon the observation, God collapses itself into everything. Black holes, stars, trees, humans, time....

Finally we come to omniscience. We can take this in the same way as omnipotent. All that is known in any given moment, is only ever known by God. It cannot be that there's a fella with a gown and crown, burdened with a colossal brain big enough to hold the library of all possible and impossible knowledge that describes all of time. It can be much more simple.

God is the knowing, the consciousness, found in every experience of knowing anything at all. God is not limited to any object known, but is both the known and the knowing. So omniscient is perhaps better translated as, 'all the knowing that is, is God'.

Rather than the image of God as a being who is Omnipresent, omnipotent and omniscient, we could phrase it rather that God is omnipresence, omnipotence, and omniscience. Though of course, these concepts are essentially education tools, and aren't supposed to be borders or limits to the scope of God.

I'm not sure if it's of interest to you, dear reader, but I think it may be of some importance to note that I am not a member of any organised religion. I am not trying to trick atheists into believing in a god and I am not trying to destroy the beliefs of the religious. It just seems to me, that perhaps it's time to really look at what humanity believes and address any dissonance in our beliefs. To truly be resolved of conflict we can't be so determined to define and separate reality, and then each other from one another. That goes for the physical and spiritual concepts we have.

Perhaps this may go some way towards bridging the pointless divide that has been created between humans in the form of different religions. All religions, as it appears to me at any rate, are fundamentally about trying to protect and carry through time, the same fundamental truth. Whether you call it meditation or prayer, Allah or Buddha, there is the goal of communion with the fundamental nature of reality.

Once this union is known, the method used to 'arrive' at this point is also seen to be of little consequence. There are an uncountable number of ways in which one may come to total union as God. We don't need to have one religion, but recognise that all religions are trying to point in the same direction. The method by which one realises God as the totality and so necessarily as oneself devoid of any concept of true 'otherness,' doesn't really matter as long as you're not hurting other living beings.

Yes, it might seem an odd moral declaration to add 'as long as you're hurting other living beings,' but it's quite sensible. If you are hurting another and spreading fear, you are fuelling the belief in separation within them. By increasing the belief in separation you are - at least through the lens of belief - taking them away from union and in that, away from God. Away from their true self and into a belief in a fictional, separate, isolated and individual self as reality: the spread of ignorance.

I still have a lot to reflect on here as the schisms between religions are complex; but I thought, at this juncture, it might be interesting to take note of where this seems to lead. If after all, God is knowing and known, then regardless of *what or how* God knows, God is always God. Although, there is little doubt that knowing oneself as a limited and threatened isolated individual produces the response of fear and suffering. When not limited by such constructs, there is peace and happiness. How else could prisoners feel free in prison and free men feel trapped by riches?

It may be the ignorant notions of a strange ape on a ball of rock rolling around a spherical fire somewhere out in the impossibly large cosmic void; or it may be a truth that pervades all of reality; or it may be somewhere in between; but it does appear as though the increase of suffering for oneself is avoided, as shown by the actions of every living being. Whereas happiness and peace seem to be what every action is geared toward expanding.

Many actions that are believed to bring peace and happiness can be relative actions - relative to the knowledge of the individual. How, for example, can someone raised in an exclusively violent environment learn how to communicate non-violently? How can they know *other,* than simply to weigh up potential violent outcomes and choose the one of least possible suffering for themselves?

A violent action may seem pointlessly violent for someone raised in more peaceful circumstances, and here enters the notion of privilege; a privilege of experience. Violence in gangs and cartels and mobs are perhaps violence based in a fear that suffering will come to them otherwise. "If I don't injure, hurt, kill, it will happen to me," "If I'm not the alpha, I might get hurt by the one who *is* the alpha". It is a misguided attempt to bring more peace to one's own life. Misguided because violence begets more violence.

Of course, if we use this logic to say that everyone should simply stop being violent, 'turn the other cheek' sort of deal, we can very easily end up with totalitarianism. We end up with the most ignorant human, the one most resistant, the last one to learn the lesson of peace, just killing everyone and assuming total domination over a population. But there are different ways to handle the transition. Turning the other cheek does not mean turning a blind eye.

What to do about totalitarianism is certainly a topic for another book entirely, but it does not seem to me that fighting it with violence is the *best* way to secure a peaceful future. The best way must be education, enlightenment over ignorance. If soldiers were aware that every human they kill is only adding to the violence, not stopping it; and that every human they kill is killing only themselves, I wonder how many soldiers there would be. If there are no soldiers, there are no humans to follow orders to commit violence. This goes for 'official government' military soldiers and police as it does for soldiers in gang warfare - institutional violence or social violence.

Education that there is a way to deep, true, lasting and tangible peace at the center of every human being is perhaps, in the common era, the most needed education there is.

To educate a population to see that they are the totality itself manifest here, to see that their nature is peace and love, would effectively destroy the current societal model of class hierarchy and the pursuit of power. What would power be used for? This power is always power *over* something else, influence over another life. Why? What for? Satisfaction? How could one be satisfied knowing their actions were causing the enslavement and suffering of others? What would be the need of satisfaction of that kind? To what end? One is already happy. One is already peaceful.

The only thing left to do would be to enlighten others to this same truth about themselves. This would be a society truly based around a foundation of freedom and liberty. It would not steal and then sell freedom back to you. It would say from the start, "You are free! Let us show you the ways in which you may feel trapped so that you may avoid them, for the sake of your own wellbeing first and foremost."

A society based around God in *this* way is a free society. A society not ruled by dogmas and restrictions, commandments and fear of punishment. Many religions *became* totalitarian as time went on. Perhaps because their central figure and the truth this figure was trying to express became obscured through multiple translations by humans who did not understand, or used it for selfish political gain. We can speculate. But regardless of the reason, it seems abundantly clear that using threat to manipulate people into behaving in a particular way is not going to lead to a more loving world, only a more fearful one.

II

GRAVITATION

A spontaneous radiating Timeform appears.

If there is only one form, the notion of directing or moving it elsewhere becomes nonsensical. It will merely emanate Time into eternity until it eventually fades away, leaving no trace behind. There's a certain beauty to this process. However, when we consider direction, it is a relative concept that requires at least two entities for relativity to exist. So, let's imagine that two Time-forms emerge, both spontaneously radiating.

A   *B*

Now we can consider the proximity between these two in terms of a 'distance.' We can establish a measurement by assigning the diameter of one sphere as '1 Unit' (1U). Based on this, we can determine that the spheres are approximately 8U apart from each other.

Additionally, we know that they're both radiating time-energy, which we can conceptualise like this:

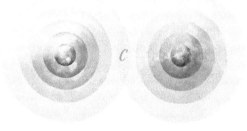

As both forms continue to radiate, there comes a point where their emitted time-energy begins to overlap, which is represented by the slightly darker spot at point C. At this overlapping region, the concentration of time-energy increases as it is continuously being added by the ongoing radiation from both A and B.

As time-energy becomes denser at point C, we can draw a connection to the concept of energy density. Drawing on Einstein's insights, we observe that as energy density increases, both length and time contract. Consequently, the measurement unit (U) between A and B decreases. In this case, the distance between them may reduce to approximately 6U.

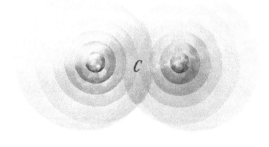

However, it's important to note that the radiation of time remains constant, resulting in a continuous increase in time-energy at point C. This further contributes to the reduction in distance between the two forms.

As the expanse of Time at point C contracts, it implies a contraction of "space" as well. This contraction manifests as the apparent movement of A and B towards each other, accelerating as Time becomes denser. Even before A and B physically combine, their unification begins to emerge at point C.

At a critical threshold, there will be a point where separating A and B would require an immense amount of Time-energy exerted from opposing sides simultaneously. Their pairing reaches a stage where pulling on one of them would result in the other being pulled along, as if they are already acting as a unified entity. The closer they get to one another, the faster they appear to move - they 'accelerate.' Acceleration occurs here because the closer point C is to the source (A and B), the greater the DENSITY of time-energy radiated into point C.

They are more or less inseparable at ₂U (above). A and B radiate their time into their union. It appears as if they sacrifice themselves, giving all their energy to the collision of two. A marriage of the gods, as two become one:

Looking at this through the philosophical lens established in Rebirth, we see that there is no distinct entity or *thing* that transforms into another entity. There is no identifiable object at the center that emits all this Time. Instead, there is the spontaneous vibration and radiation of Time itself. There is no center and no circumference; there exists only a subtle gradient that gives rise to the concept of time and location. It is only a continuous flow.

Depending on how we view this flowing gradient, we will see different realities, just like how two people can view one event, and while one may get offended, the other may laugh uninhibited. Here arises two different perspectives - two different realities - from one event: Objects enacting process, or process enacting objects.

The Black Hole

The Black Hole presents a perplexing challenge within the modern understanding of physics, particularly when it comes to comprehending what lies beyond its boundary, known as the event horizon. The conventional explanation suggests that the event horizon functions as a surface of a celestial object possessing immense gravitational force, so strong that even light can't escape its pull. However, I'm suggesting there is no object acting on a separate fabric of spacetime, there is simply the contraction/expansion process. This necessarily implies that there is no 'singularity' as in, "A point-like object with zero size" that is somehow finite, yet has 'infinite properties' such as infinite density, infinite gravity and so on. The singularity is only a limitation of the language of mathematics, not a limitation of reality.

What does it mean for black holes and the event horizon if there is no physical center? It would mean, from the point of view of this schema at least, that the event horizon is not the edge of some object beneath, but a primordial boundary of pure time creation from the infinity of existence itself. It is a boundary of our perception, not of reality.

It is a *moment*, not a *thing* - a moment of spontaneous Time amidst infinite Being. Therefore, given all that we have discovered, the moment of a black hole *must* be conscious in some way, as a moment of self-observation of existence itself.

Beyond that horizon of perception therefore, we won't be able to find any *thing* at all for there is no process that exists outside of Time. Aiming towards the center, an immense darkness envelopes experience, as all that is present, is the crushing gravitas of emerging Time. Pure Time, a seeming eternity of it, drawing the entire universe into its eye of perception, simultaneous with the expansion of itself as an ever-compounding observation of infinity.

Stephen Hawking created a theoretical framework for the disappearance or 'evaporation' of black holes, which, incidentally, is called Hawking *Radiation*. It would take billions upon billions upon billions of times longer than the current age of the universe for a black hole to evaporate according to the calculations, but the theory is interesting. It says that the virtual particle pairs (+ and -) theorised in quantum mechanics, come into and out of existence on the edge of the event horizon. Sometimes, a 'negative energy particle' will 'fall in' to the black hole and this would allow the positive one to escape and become a 'real particle'. The negative energy particle would reduce the overall energy of the black hole, and the positive one would maintain the balance of the energy of the universe, 'radiating' out into space. The positively charged particles would radiate mostly as the massless particle of light, a photon.

It's going to seem quite audacious of me, but I'm going to reframe this.

Radiation

The radiation of light also makes the most sense in the framework I am offering because light has no tick, it is, in a sense, timeless. Light is always instantaneous, yet, it appears as if relative. It appears as if it takes around eight minutes for light to travel from the Sun to Earth for example, but that is only from this relative perspective on Earth. From light's perspective 'spacetime' contracts to length o and time o. For light, there is neither space nor time. From light's point of view, the leaf on the tree on planet Earth absorbs it at the same moment that it is emitted from the atoms constituting the Sun. And this is true regardless how far away the two points of emission and absorption are.

This is my first point. This note on light goes to further explain the blackness of black holes, as light is not observed (by us at least) except through reflection whereby it enters relativity. If it was known *without* reflection then space would not be black, it would be a flood of blinding light! It isn't blinding light because it is not known in the traveling, as light doesn't 'travel'. It is never on a journey.

Since a black hole has no 'solid' surface, there isn't anything to *reflect* the abundant light radiating from it and so, it appears as if black. I'm hypothesising that this blackness is, paradoxically, the *source* of all light, and it is black because light does not illumine itself.

One could argue that our conventional understanding of light is actually the result of infinite energy potential refracting through the medium of observation and collapsing into perception. In other words, the illumination we refer to as 'light,' which is commonly believed to exist independently of observation is only a metaphor for the illuminating power of observation. Consciousness is that which illumines all experiences and because consciousness is the nature of infinite Being, when there is an observation of itself this blinding light is released as the collapse of eternity pours forth collapsing the environment around with the light of its observation. The world is Enlightened into Being.

The further away from the black hole we look, the more the radiation has a chance to reflect and so we see the 'emergence of photons'. This 'emergence' is simply Time interacting (or 'interfering') with itself and what is emerging is apparent separation via perception.

Further to this, all the radiation that comes from the black hole (or indeed any object) does not necessarily transform into photons, it may simply remain as a sort of 'expanding time-wave'. Time, as it radiates away from a black hole for example (or a star or planet and so on) may simply be generating a time-gradient environment. What this means is that the further away from the center and into space you look, the further back in time you'd see because you would necessarily be looking at *previous* 'waves' of time.

Following the gradient in the reverse direction, back to yourself as the observer, you see that your viewpoint is the source of the radiation - actively pushing the environment away from you. This appears outwardly as an expanding environment, and inwardly an ever-vanishing point of observation from which you are looking (*like* a singularity).

If physicists are looking for something that would act both as a scene of expansion and as a means of gravitation, this radiating time hypothesis appears to describe the mysterious process of 'Dark Energy' (though it need not be bound by such ideas).

Dark energy is said to surround all galaxies and, given that there are supermassive black holes at the center of every galaxy, it makes sense if they are radiating Time on such a gargantuan scale.

It is perhaps also sensible to say that there are 'frequencies' of Time-radiation creating a gradient of time around celestial objects. This movement would generate the appearance of expanding distances between galaxies and as described at the beginning, simultaneously be responsible for their attraction.

Falling In - Information Paradox

As a black hole is not an object, does anything really 'fall in'? Let's say you find yourself falling towards it. When you pass the event horizon, you will disappear. Of course, right? Whatever complexity you are will be contracted to zero as time intervals flatten to trillions of years encapsulated in the most microscopic of moments. You will cease to be what you were as the complex organism that built the spaceship to get itself there. However, this is where we run into what is called 'The Information Paradox'.

The question is put from a computing-mind perspective, namely that all 'quanta' - measurable units - of reality carry 'information' and when absorbed into the black hole, we do not know where all this information goes. To make this a little easier, we can substitute the term 'information' - retaining the same meaning - for 'knowledge'. The knowledge contained in DNA for example, rather than the 'information' or 'bits' contained in DNA.

The term 'information' or 'bits' is favoured because it is a term used for computers, for machines, and the current narrative of most scientific endeavour is that existence is mechanical - Newtonian, non-intelligent of itself, yet brings about the illusion of intelligence through quantum machinery.

If we look at this problem of 'The *Knowledge* Paradox', what is being asked is the same question humanity is asking about death. Where does the information contained in a star go, should it fall into the black hole? Where does knowledge go when we die? These two are the same question. Is it really the end or will I be saved in some way? - Preserved? Humanity is trying to figure out what it has never been able to figure out and no matter how many different avenues it has tried to go down over the many thousands of years it has been struggling with this, it cannot do it from the same point of view it refuses to give up on: that of a finite life. It is this point of view that it is worried about losing precisely because it believes finitude is the basis of reality. The belief is the fear. How interesting.

There are many ideas for solutions to the information paradox; one such idea is that all the information/knowledge is stored on the surface of the black hole as if the black hole is a celestial computer. This is called the holographic principle, believed to be the case that all the information on the surface of the black hole is two-dimensional but projects a three-dimensional world.

In psychology there is that same term 'projection' but it means thrusting the thoughts of the brain into the environment and believing them to come from the environment rather than from you. Is there an equivalency here?

We, humanity, are sure that the brain has all the folds on its two-dimensional surface to increase the surface area so that more information, that is, knowledge, can be stored there. Aren't we also sure that without the brain, none of this environment would be perceived at all? - That we see only what is processed and projected, or, reflected, by the brain? So it should come as no surprise that there is a hologram theory of black holes because we have a hologram theory of the brain. What seems to be happening for humanity is projection of thought and the attempt to figure thought as if that is the ultimate fundamental nature of reality.

There is a projection of the human, mechanistic understanding of a brain onto the universe.

Then we run into a paradox as the brain is asked how it can preserve itself when faced with death. Where does the knowledge accumulated in life go upon death, and where does the knowledge/information that falls into a black hole go?

Some of the answer to both of these questions may be hidden in Quantum Mechanics. Everywhere you go, you communicate and interact with the environment around you, leaving an impression. You 'entangle' with it. That communication, the trail of entanglement that you leave, is your legacy. It's not the deathbed that matters most, it's not the final moment of achievement, it's all of it - including the whole trail of entanglement that lead you to that point. That reverberation in and through Time is where the knowledge of who and what you were and are, is 'stored'.

What we refer to as death, is the moment that all resonances held in the body from a lifetime of communication are released back into the environment.[37] In the physical death, all the vibrations you held, all the vibrations you lived, will, as entropy suggests, reverberate or dissipate out of the body as it decays back into the environment.

So what about the black hole? Does it hold or maintain anything? It seems to me that whatever is contracted to zero at the event horizon is renewed. It is energy stripped of its old vibration habit, its old complexity, and in however many millions upon billions of years, it will be radiated back out again as pure Time. We see a similar thing every spring that after death comes new life. It's not the same life as before, but it is influenced by the lives before. Even the environment the new life travels through is an environment shaped by previous lives.

In this way you absolutely *can* meet your ancestors in the environment around you, not in their old body, but embodied in the environment they affected. Religious pilgrimages are this exact same idea: travel to the place that was so profoundly affected by such a wondrous and wise human and then live in something similar to their presence, even if only a little. This is, essentially, knowledge of entanglement, and it's down to unstoppable and relentless communication between every aspect of existence simultaneously.

White Holes

A black hole is said to be an event that you cannot exit, one that only absorbs energy. It is said (in one instance) to be an event that persists into an eternal future. A white hole is the mathematical opposite of this and is perfectly well accepted

---

[37] This is something that can be done before the physical death. It's partly what psychotherapy is all about: releasing old tension-habits.

under General Relativity, it has just never been recorded. A white hole is an event that you cannot enter, one that only emits energy. It is said (in one instance) to be an event that persists from the eternal past.

But let's come to the holistic perspective and look again because if a black hole is always radiating Time, then these two opposites of white or black hole are in fact the exact same phenomenon seen from two different angles. It's as if one of them is looking in a mirror, but which one is the reflection, and which one the reality?

Physics at the moment is enjoying the idea of a symmetrical universe, and that seems to be because symmetry is the demonstration of itself, by itself; it seems balanced. When you see yourself in a mirror you can say, "*There* I am," whereas before you said, "*Here* I am". You can externalise yourself in a way. But you are, nevertheless, looking at the same phenomenon that is looking, only from a different perspective.

If the equation can be reversed, then might it be because it's the same event seen from opposite angles? Not spatial angles, temporal angles: the angles of Past and Future. If what we're describing is seen to be going into the future, we're looking from the past. If what we're describing seems to be going into the past, we're looking from the future. Past and future define each other because they too are reflections of one another.

Like the white hole, the black hole cannot be entered because there is no *thing* to be entered. It is pure observation; infinite conscious being. The black hole also cannot be exited for the same reason. The event horizon is simultaneously destruction and creation - eternal rebirth. Because no *process*, no *particular pattern of resonance* can arrive without being collapsed, there is no process or particular pattern of resonance that leaves it either. Any Time that is radiated, from the point of view of the black hole, doesn't 'travel through' the past to meet the present and go on into the future at all. From the black hole's perspective it *is* the eternal presence of reality. It is the creator of past and future in exactly the same way the human being is, purely by virtue of observing itself.

The outward radiation of Time-energy and the inward pulling of time-forms are two perspectives of the same event. Gravity is simultaneous with Time-radiation. The endless outpouring of colossal amounts of energy from the white hole *is* the eternal outpouring of the black hole. The relentless pulling-in of astronomical amounts of energy from the black hole is the nature of the white hole due to its own unimaginable energy. They are one, they are a black-white *whole*. Appearing different, yet the same.[38]

Patterns are created through relationship and interaction. Different types of interaction at different scales result in different phenomena surrounding the 'black-white whole'. At one scale it may be a planet, at another, a star, at another, a galaxy, at another, an atom. This 'quantum vacuum energy' of "particles popping in and out of existence" may well be happening at all scales. Enormous black holes may be the same event happening at galactic scales, the quantum vacuum may be it happening at quantum scales. Perhaps all of this, what we call 'The Universe' is it happening at a *universal* scale. Perhaps every event, every moment, is universes inside universes. Worlds within worlds within worlds...

---

[38] Isn't it interesting that the Yin-Yang symbol of Taoism is this exact representation of relationship? Black in the white and white in the black, no true opposition, one complete unified motion.

Time Gradients

If we take this to a smaller scale of Earth, we can see that this phenomenon is a Time gradient in and of itself. Different complexities of process are able to occur in a small distance. From the Earth's core we would have this same 'black whole' event but absolutely minute by comparison to a galactic-scale appearance. Energy is intense at the center and gently eases off and becomes what we call 'rock'. Then appearances like organisms and water; then a gentle drifting off into gases as the atmosphere thins and dissipates; then a time gradient, or, 'the curving of spacetime'.

External objects coming into this Time gradient of Earth such as asteroids, are forced through Time. They are broken down as they go through a huge increase in its local entropy; set ablaze as the energy is accelerated!

The potential of existence is so vast, but this model of Time radiation can be applied in other areas to explain many other phenomena. Gravitational lensing for instance is made sense of through density of the emerging Time-gradient and reflection of light through this density, adding 'temporal reality' to light, appearing to slow it down in a relative sense, not an absolute sense. So its path appears altered.

Gravitational Lensing

Gradient 1
Diameter

Gradient 2
Spin Drag

If there is sufficient interest in exploring more, another more specific book can be published addressing more questions or potential complications. I feel however, that what has been gone over so far may well suffice to allow the imagination to run away with this and naturally and effortlessly interpret more phenomena for yourself.

'Gravitation' is magic clothed in a lab coat. Time is the great spell, the fantastic illusion that supposes itself to be fundamental reality. See through this illusion. See that all objects are only Time, and see that for all the time-forms, these are but patterns of process. This process is only the movement of Infinite Being. The Hindus may say: 'It is only Brahman that moves'; the Abrahamic religions might say: 'It is only God that moves in Himself, as Himself'; the Buddhists, 'It is only Buddha that does all this'; the non-denominational philosopher may say: 'All is only the movement of Being'. Despite the diverse terminology, these statements are synonymous, conveying the underlying concept that everything in existence undivided. That existence is unity in an ever-unfolding cosmic dance of celebration to its own magnificence.

Evolution

By now, it's clear that the conventional narrative surrounding species adaptation does not fully align with the theory presented in this book. It is not a denial of evolution; rather, it calls for a fresh examination of the facts, free from the fear-driven narrative of survival and competition that often accompanies them. This unified theory invites us to reevaluate the common understanding of evolution, stripping away the limiting perspectives to explore an alternate interpretation.

The fact is that organisms change. Further, they change in ways reflective of the environment in which they live. For the same reason we don't see giraffes changing in a way that would mean they could hold their breath underwater, we don't see penguins changing to reach leaves on the higher branches of trees. These changes would not be reflective of the environment out of which the organisms as we know them, emerge.

Over the course of millions of years, incremental changes occurring in each generation accumulate to such an extent that they bring about profound transformations in organisms, making them almost unrecognisable compared to their distant ancestors. This fundamental principle lies at the heart of the theory of evolution.

The *reason* why this is thought to happen is the narrative that is attached to it. The narrative that accompanies the theory of evolution is in two parts. First, it attributes these changes to *random* mutation, disrupting what would otherwise be presumed as successive 'carbon copies' - ironically enough. Second, fear is presented as the driving force behind the actions of organisms. This fear is sometimes framed as the ultimate threat of death, thus giving rise to the central theme in the modern narrative surrounding evolution (and so life itself): the notion of relentless fearful competition among individuals, each striving to secure their own survival.

Of course, this reasoning is incomplete, for eternal survival is ultimately impossible for an individual. No thing can endure indefinitely. Every organism, every object, *will* experience its own death. Death marks the culmination, the cessation - from the human perspective at least - of that particular form's journey. It may be perceived as a finality, or perhaps, akin to a ship vanishing over the horizon, it continues in a way that lies beyond our sensory perceptions. I don't possess firsthand knowledge, as I am not dead (at the time of writing this at least); though the notion of finality smacks of finitude and there appears to be no *inherent* quality of 'finality' in existence.

This narrative of competition to survive is to condemn every living being, and indeed life itself, to be essentially moronic. To chase after an impossibility as the ultimate goal of life...

It could be argued that animals are not consciously aware of their participation in this pursuit, while we, with our 'superior intelligence,' have stepped outside of this game. However, if animals are not aware of the narrative of indefinite survival as their particular form, then what is their experience? What drives their actions and physical changes if they are not guided by fear and competition?

Charles Darwin mentioned in his autobiography that all animals appear to be in *search* of happiness, reflecting his understanding of their behaviours and motivations. However, it is possible that his cultural background and the historical context in which he lived influenced his interpretation. Living in a time marked by fear and challenges, Darwin may have viewed happiness as a desired state amidst a reality believed to be made of adversity and competition. Nonetheless, he recognised that animals not only exhibited fear responses, but also acted in ways suggestive of a pursuit of happiness or well-being.

If we think about it for a moment, perhaps this is more obvious than it initially seemed. Why would anyone run from fear? It must be because there is a comparison, a weighing of options, a contemplation however momentary, that turns into the decision to move the organism away from certain stimulus and towards others. The perfect counter-balance for fear is peace, love and happiness. Disorder is avoided, and order is preferred.

So if we are transfixed by and centred around happiness rather than the appearance of fear, might we have a different view of evolution entirely?

Centred around happiness, the view of evolution is that everything evolves and changes in a way that moves away from temporary fear and disharmony, all the while moving towards a proliferation of maximum possible happiness. For some reason, humans often neglect to explicitly acknowledge the role of happiness in the way it shapes their lives, despite it being fundamental to being human.

No individual willingly pursues something unless they believe, in some way, that it will lead to happiness or peace. However, we might question why some humans find themselves in abusive relationships, which seemingly contradict the pursuit of peace and happiness. From the perspective of someone who recognises that abusive relationships are not conducive to the proliferation of happiness, such actions appear counterintuitive. Yet, for individuals trapped in the cycle of abuse and feelings of unworthiness, they may perceive a sense of maximum equilibrium (and an imagined state of peace) when their internal mental state aligns with their external environment. This alignment creates a semblance of order, even though it may not genuinely lead to lasting peace and happiness.

The mind made of abusive narratives will not be at peace (initially) in a harmonious and loving environment. The mind is at odds with the environment and this is confusing. Being confused about your environment for an organism *must* illicit fear because it means there is a distinction, a separation between the organism and the environment and so, potentially, death. This may be why, when children live in an abusive home, they are scared. Their innate happiness is in contradiction to the environment, and as a natural response, they adapt by learning the nature of the environment in order to act in ways that mitigate pain, fear, and suffering.

It is worth considering whether the fear of death is not primarily rooted in the unknown nature of dying, but rather in the feeling of life being inherently incongruent with itself—the total absence of peace. Fear, then, becomes the movement of the organism to seek a space (or indeed time) where this incongruence is dissolved. Hence, Darwin (and many others) would see a 'movement towards happiness,' and so make happiness a goal to be reached. The turning around of this perspective sees happiness and harmony as the natural state and fear and disorder as temporary moments of disequilibrium. This perception of disequilibrium is the self-same perception of a distinction between two entities: self and other, organism and environment.

The process of attempting to maintain equilibrium between the mental state/individual self and the environment potentially is and has been, for billions of years, the process of evolution. The attempt to comprehend the environment in such a way that the organism can be at total peace with it; be ONE with it; BE it. As Earth moves through its orbit and through the milky way, it changes. Asteroids, temperature, solar winds, magnetic fields, all of this alters the planet and in turn, the organisms begin to perceive a sense of disequilibrium and so adaptation takes place to dissolve it. Of course, when some species adapt in ways that mean other species are now seen as food, that other species will respond to that disequilibrium.

If an organism is apparently fundamentally at odds with its environment it cannot understand itself. If an organism cannot understand itself it dies in fear, sooner or later. Depending upon the severity of its change of environment, it may be an immediate fearful death, such as plonking a penguin in the middle of the Serengeti as it is 'chased' by lions with no ocean to escape away into. Or, it may be prolonged and involve more mental anguish, such as placing a plains and forest dwelling hominid amidst one hundred square miles or so of concrete, exhaust fumes, and the expectation that everything *should* be okay.

In the latter condition, mental health would be expected to take a nosedive, as the organism must somehow try to live abstractly in order to make sense of its environment, feeling unable to escape the strangeness of it. This abstraction of the self is the use of the mind for self-understanding and, given that the mind is a tool for memory, memory manipulation, and an attempt to predict the future (a lot of which is based on fear), to maintain an identity founded in the simulated self brought about through a perception of disequilibrium, is to be entirely unstable.

Within this context, humans tend to identify themselves as fictional constructs within their own imagination. Then the question of what happens after death arises. This is the concern arising out of the ignorance of the simulated self, dependent upon the body that it cannot understand. It essentially asks, "What happens when my host dies?" as it is entirely made of the notion that it is *other* than a function of the body.

Viewing reality through the lens of separation perpetuates this understanding, characterised by fear, linear time, isolation, distinction, the mind-body problem, and numerous other divisive ideas. Human cultures may only cement this ignorance with every further conclusion as they could begin to claim that individuals are the cause and reason for waning mental health, not the change of environment. Instead of interest and investigation, blame is often cast onto the separate individual, further isolating the sense of separation, and further exacerbating the problem.

Through the lens of equilibrium, we see that the declining mental health in societies, particularly capitalist ones, is not an anomaly but a reflection of the system itself. It challenges us to view mental health issues as systemic imbalances rather than individual shortcomings. By addressing the societal structures that generate disequilibrium, we can flourish in the harmonious environment the human animal is naturally aligned with.

Equilibrium is the name of the game.

*

As a reflection of the environment, organisms *are* the environment. Note the simple truth that no organism anywhere or any-when, has ever come from outside reality, outside Being. Every organism *emerges* from the environment of Being we could say. Animals, plants, fungi, whatever categories we want to create, they do not instantaneously materialise from somewhere other than reality, they *grew out of* the environment. Accepting this, it seems very little could stand in the way of coming to the logical conclusion that, fundamentally, the organisms are the environment as they are entirely made of it. There is no *real* distinction, only a superficial one.

It's only in the belief that we are an organism and *not* the environment that there is a divide. Drop that belief. You are the environment and there is no *actual* divide. You cannot escape the environment of infinity - you *are* IT.

If we then look back towards change over time, we see that the organisms change *with* the environment, not in contradiction to it. The elephant changes to have smaller tusks or none at all, due to the environment of humans killing those with bigger tusks. This change is not fear and it isn't 'random mutation'. It's call and response, it's reflection, it's relationship, it's intelligence.

We can say that the hunters don't kill those with smaller tusks and so they survive and pass on that gene to their offspring and that's why smaller tusks are more prevalent now. Yes. We can say that too. But it doesn't take away that the environment is reflected in the organism and vice versa. Again, equilibrium. It has become, due to the action of humans, disharmonious for a male elephant to have large tusks. Movement towards harmony, peace, and equilibrium with the environment, has lead to smaller tusks.

At the time when tusks developed to be larger, the main threats to an elephant's happiness were likely only other male elephants or big cats like lionesses moving as a group. Large tusks would seriously injure and so likely deter lionesses and lions, and, in the same way, deter other male elephants. The larger the tusks, the more likely it was that the male elephant would be safer from conflict. Thus they would find their life to be more peaceful and harmonious overall.[39]

Now, humans, or more precisely rifles, are their main threat. Larger tusks are actually a disadvantage now, so much so that life in fact *ends* because of it. The organism's happiness stops. How can that behaviour of growing large tusks continue if there is no happiness to be found in it?

Here is a profound moment of reflection, I feel: Life is not growing into suffering; life is growing into happiness.

There may be moments of suffering, but this needn't be feared or chastised as those moments only help to define the behaviours of happiness.

The suffering of a human being is seen very directly as the limited knowledge it has in terms of possible behaviours. Never forget that babies know almost nothing. They nevertheless seem to be capable of immense happiness and tranquillity within themselves. This knowing of almost nothing doesn't limit them in their experience of happiness. They are not born as consistently suffering bundles of atoms until human culture graces them with the true knowledge of how to be happy. They are already capable of happiness. How could this be the case if it must be pursued? Happiness needn't be pursued if it is natural to the baby, it need only be realised. That is why the

---

[39] Is there a similarity in why humans wanted to own these tusks? Safety? Even if only for an image? - Perhaps, perhaps not, but intriguing nonetheless.

phrase 'self-realisation' is used in Hinduism and Advaita Vedanta. You simply realise the nature of yourself, and realise the happiness and peace that it is.

We are not taught how to be happy; we are taught how to suffer.

This is disastrous for an economy geared towards selling you happiness. Capitalism, or in its less limited conceptual form - as Guy DeBord phrased it - 'The Spectacle' feeds on selling your nature back to you, and so works to keep its population ignorant of their own nature.

Being taught to suffer is not exclusive to human political ideologies or economies; political ideologies and economies are simply the use of that phenomenon to provide an advantage to one group or another. If happiness is the natural way of life, then being taught to suffer is the only possible way to suffer. Happiness or peace being fundamental, there is no way to *learn* how to be happy. You already are happy, to the confusion of those who suffer.

Suffering is like a flag post or a signal that reverberates through the organism (something we may call a reflex) making it aware that the actions being taken are not leading to happiness - causing a change in behaviour. This is adaptation at a small timescale.

We must climb down from our intellectual high horses here and see that the knowledge contained within the entire human organism, gathered over millions of years of experience, *far* outweighs the trivial knowledge learned in a single human lifetime. The body as a whole knows more than any individual division *could* know - memories of the brain included. Suffering is momentary and ordinarily, when listened to, would cause immediate movement away from the stimulus and a return to peacefulness.

Curiosity though, and an increased ability to see across more distant temporal horizons, can allow us to 'suffer' something uncomfortable at the beginning, knowing it to be a route to a more stable or indeed an entirely different expanse of happiness that is perhaps more long term, or even simply a more apparent happiness. Examples include beginning an exercise regime, eating less sugar, therapy, a meditation practice, even just being honest with people can be uncomfortable if you're not used to it. Honesty though, both with others and oneself, is certainly a happiness not found in endless indulgence in sense pleasures.

The reason suffering is taken from discomfort in a given moment, or in adjustment to a healthier equilibrium, and is instead perpetuated in every day life seems to be because we rely on that intellectual knowledge of a single lifetime to teach us the path to that distant, far away happiness. That intellectual knowledge is what we've learned. Although it isn't all exclusively stories of suffering - that would drive the organism mad, surely - it *is* often trained to project happiness *onto* mental objects. Happiness comes to be believed to be *in* those memories, and then there is the attempt to repeat those experiences. Our experiences are confused for the happiness that we are. If you check your happiest memories, they will, I wager, be memories of times when you felt no expectations on you, no drive to be somewhere else, no drive to be someone else, but you were free to simply be. You found your inner baby!

So why might we feel like happiness is not the nature of ourselves? It must be because we find ourselves suffering more than we find ourselves peaceful and happy. Why then are we suffering?

When action is taken to maintain what has been taught - the tradition mindset - it may be the case that what you have been taught was not beneficial for the intrinsic happiness of *every* organism, but only for the satisfaction of desires of a *particular* organism. That particular organism may be a teacher or a parent for example, and they might have punished you into acting in ways that stop them from feeling discomfort, believing happiness to be found in *particular* circumstances. They try to control you into being their perfect environment for happiness, unaware that *they* are already the perfect environment for happiness.

Doing this conditions children into feeling their happiness is not as important as keeping up expectations of others. Thus enters a struggle, as the child believes their happiness negatively impacts the happiness of others.

It is, in my experience, an accurate observation that being that unconditional happiness and peace may well upset somebody else. It could be called jealousy, but it's perhaps more holistic to see it instead as the suffering that is performed as the environment of happiness is now perceived to be in disequilibrium with the internal environment of suffering.

Being confronted with happiness is confusing to suffering and it can't escape except to either leave, or to again, try to control your happiness into being suffering so that there is once again the (facade) of peace through the perception of equilibrium.

Happiness is, in truth, not a cause of suffering. Like when someone begins to eat less sugar or stops smoking, there *can* be (though not always) the adjustment period that feels painful. But, over time, the feeling of not smoking, or of eating less or no added sugar, or of being surrounded by happiness, will rebalance in the organism and a new equilibrium will be reached. This equilibrium will be one of a greater sense of the happiness of one's own being. This is why great care must be taken in removing a dependency such as smoking or sugar or, yes, suffering, so as not to simply become dependent upon something else.

The game of dependency confuses the organism. It must believe itself to suffer fundamentally and herein lies the saviour complex. A god or being will come from outside and save me, the one who suffers. But, these gods, imbuing you with the free will that you will hopefully use to worship them, cannot manipulate that free will to save you from yourself. It is within the realms of free will to suffer.

But suffering is not a choice; suffering is merely a habit. It is a habit of behaviour enacted through mental conditioning and patterns. When we look to those patterns to inform us about potential actions in any given situation, the baby that had no intellectual knowledge of human cultures can only have learned what it was taught by others. Therefore if the organism is to check its memory banks for potential actions, it can only select from knowledge it has collected. If all it has collected are behaviours and habits that move it towards suffering, it can act on the balance of *'the lesser of two evils'*.

Over time, as humanity has discovered with research into learning, humans will stop taking the time to weigh up options, simply skipping to the most well known and well used option. It seems as if it is imagined to be a 'necessary evil' in order to reach happiness afterwards.

When humans declare themselves creatures of habit, they are declaring themselves under the authority and reign of habit. All it takes is a moment where new behaviours are seen to be possible or a new perspective is presented that resonates somewhere in their being, for the habit to be questioned. The whole process is automatic. All it takes is a change of environment and, in that change, alternate options, alternate lifestyles, alternate beliefs, and alternate perspectives are made known to the organism as at least *possible*.

When it is known to be possible that there could be some happiness that is not dependent upon circumstance, some happiness that is intrinsic, that is self-generated as the nature of what you are, that *is* what you are, the habit is already beginning to inoculate the pattern of suffering from the inside out.

Suffering is the habit of behaving in accordance with the belief that there is a path to happiness and you must first walk its distance.

This journey is that of happiness, denying to itself that it exists now so that it may journey to a place where it feels it may finally be able to be itself.

We see the evolution of mind with the evolution of matter here. The evolution of the self-defensive mind, imagining it protects happiness by reacting to fear and suffering through reflection. The body perceives the pain of fear and suffering and acts from and *as* the world it perceives. It tries to protect itself by either attacking the stimulus, running from it, freezing in its presence or appeasing it or a mixture of these actions. The mind anticipates, and, its reality being that of memory, it reacts in the same way even toward *ideas* believed to cause suffering or happiness. Then we get mental suffering such as anxiety, which is, as mind and matter are the same process, a form of physical suffering.

It is the outlook with which humans are being conditioned - that of fear and separation as fundamental - that is, I believe, a root cause of this epidemic of declining health. Humans are divorcing themselves from themselves, and then pursuing themselves believing only a future version of themselves will be happy with themselves. The phrase found coming out of the mouths and echoing in the minds of those suffering from poor mental health is sometimes, verbatim, 'I'm broken'. This is not overly dramatic; this is a genuine reflection of the conditioning.

It is the reality witnessing itself lost in suffering; so much so that its wholeness seems to be shattered, fragmented.

Cultures operating on separation and fear provide acceptable self-images in terms of fragmentation by means of comparison. You are acceptable compared to her, they are unacceptable compared to you, *this* is what beauty looks like, *this* is what success looks like, *this* is what happiness looks like. Life is judged based on arbitrary (and ever-changing) standards imposed by society. This destructive mindset erodes diversity, whether in culture, opinions, or life experiences, as everything is homogenised. So yes, humans feel broken. The culture tells them they're broken apart into pieces, some parts acceptable and some not; or are even told that being 'broken' is not acceptable. It is no wonder, then, that humans feel broken in such a culture that fragments and devalues their inherent wholeness.

What it will take to change this is the development or re-emergence of a holistic culture that points to the wholeness of reality and the oneness of the individual with the entire process, thus dissolving the individual as a target of reward or punishment. But we needn't wait for an entire culture to erect itself around us first. See it now for yourself and be among the *creators* of this new culture. See that your evolution as the entire environment has more weight and significance than what the mean old man or woman once told you about how you *ought* to behave in circumstance *x*.

See that in the same way penguins do not evolve out of the Serengeti because the penguin is not a separation but an *expression* of the environment in which it lives, your body too is an expression of the environment in which you live. In moments when you feel at odds, or uncomfortable in the environment, just ask if it's because you're aiming towards a greater sense of your own happiness long-term, or if it's because you believe your happiness is being controlled, conditioned and manipulated to suit someone else's idea of what you *should* be to allow them to be dependent upon you.

By looking at evolution through the lens of happiness and peace as fundamental we can move away from the competitive and aggressive worldview and towards a more cooperative worldview.

Do plants compete for resources with a cold and isolated drive to dominate, all with the belief that a monoculture is the best possible outcome? Or do they cooperate with one another and with the animals, sharing nutrients, communicating through chemical signals and mycelium, and sharing their own bodies as habitats creating a diverse and thriving ecosystem? Why are animals any different? Do animals want to create a monoculture? Or can we see, even in death, a collaboration? Is it a circle of life, or a pyramid of life? Is there a dominator, a ruler, a king of life at the 'top,' looking down on others as weak and inferior? Does the shark, lion, or eagle *dominate* life? Even, does the *mycelium* dominate life? Or is there a harmonious interplay of energies in which no perceived opposition exists as a hierarchy between dominator and dominated?

The ego-centric view of physical dominance of others as mighty, right and evolutionarily superior is a tired, weary tale. It has been told since the insecurities of fearful humans were first tenuously resolved by externalising their pain, and 'power over' became a way to temporarily delay facing it. Must we continue it? For the benefit of who exactly? This competitive view of life is morbid and always puts those with the most accumulation in a seat of authority within society. Do not be mistaken, the way in which we frame nature, and life itself, is inevitably going to be the way in which we frame our culture.

So is it any wonder that something about this culture feels... inauthentic? It does not accurately reflect the natural harmony of the entire planet, the entire cosmos even. And so we feel disharmonious, the activities of this culture spread disharmony and destruction, not because we're 'bad creatures,' but because we are operating under a woefully inaccurate interpretation of ourselves and our surroundings.

By altering our framing we shift our perspective, and what we perceive is all down to our perspective. Shifting our perspective begins with looking for it. If we want to be more grateful, look for things you're grateful for. In time, you will adapt to these discoveries and your environment will reflect your mindset. You will be surrounded by not only what you are grateful for, but gratitude. You will, in turn, reflect that gratitude and you'll enter into a different kind of feedback loop. So look for the collaboration of life, look for the innocence, look for the interconnectedness, look for the happiness. You'll see, within 90 seconds of earnest looking and finding, that you'll start feeling the emotional ramifications of what you are perceiving. You won't be looking *for* it, you'll just be looking *at* it.

See that the creation of the environment is done by the organism, and the creation of the organism is done by the environment. As such, these two distinctions are unnecessary. There is simply existence, patterning itself as it perceives itself. Through what we may call incidental suffering, every living being learns how it can live in harmony with its perceptions in a way that minimises suffering and disorder, and maximises harmony and therefore, happiness.

Penguins would not be happy in the Serengeti because they are not the harmonious expression of that environment. They would be much too warm, their current diet would not be possible, and they'd have a hard time escaping predators.

Equally, giraffes would not be happy in Antarctica for similar reasons. By maintaining focus on the natural harmony, happiness and peace of existence, evolution takes place. Adaptation is the creation of ways in which stimulus that is perceived to cause pain can be minimised. Methods such as blubber in water or fur on land to minimise cold, thus allowing more ease; longer necks to reach taller branches, minimising strain, and allowing more ease; keener eyes to minimise the risk of neglectfully stubbing your toe - destroying your whole life for five to ten seconds... allowing more ease.

The bottom line is, life does not evolve as separate things *in* the environment, struggling to cope with it (bringing in all kinds of problems like abiogenesis); life *is* the environment. Life is not rare, life is what *all of this,* is! It is a joyous celebration, a cosmic collaboration of self-patterning time-energy as atoms resonate in harmony to dance as molecules, as cells sing together to create the chorus of an organ, and organs paint the masterpiece of an organism. All the apparent forms are the glorious free expression of the intrinsic peace and happiness of this miraculous infinite reality. And all of this, the entire awe-inspiring, wondrous, breathtaking, miraculous, infinite reality, is you.

META

Closing Note & Acknowledgement

First and foremost I want to thank and acknowledge you, the reader. Thank you for opening yourself up to a new perspective. Thank you for hearing what I wanted to say, and receiving what I had to give. I hope one day to return the favour.

In a circular fashion, the gratitude expressed at the beginning of this book is the gratitude expressed at the end. Truly everything that has happened has lead to this book (and many other things of course). Ultimately, there isn't anything that I am not grateful for and wish to acknowledge. If I were to include everything here however, it would take up your whole life to read it, and I'm already too late to start writing it. I've forgotten a lot of what happened, perhaps not in terms of thought patterns, but certainly in terms of event recollection.

So in that vein I simply acknowledge the nature of this art to be an expression of the entire environment. I don't really feel as if it's 'my idea'. It is simply the understanding the environment has about itself *here*. I see beauty in it, so, naturally, I want to share it. And if you're interested in a dialogue, I'd love to talk to you about it.

In terms of scientific references and references to quotes and things like that, I recommend some autodidactic research because the likelihood is, you will find something interesting that I didn't find, and now you've learned something new. Bonus. Then you can tell me about it and I can learn. Double bonus. The body of research that has gone into this book is in truth, my body, and given that I didn't take continuous notes of what I learned where, it's more or less impossible to trace everything back to its original source. Though, with research, you could very easily find information that aligns with the experiments I've been describing with reference to quantum physics for example, or you can find Thomas Nagel's *What's It Like To Be A Bat* article if you search for it, Richard R. Skemp's book is widely available etc.

Believing Unity is, in my view, more of a work of art than a scientific paper whereby all points made must be referenced to some external authority who said it first. Art thrives on creativity and moving in innovative ways. Sometimes you'll do things that you cannot reference because it is a new insight or idea. Art is an amalgam of circumstances, novel interpretation and execution. Just as when you see a painting you can see which artists from history may have influenced them, yet can appreciate new ideas and styles, here too you may be able to see influences from other philosophers and scientists as well as original ideas. Such is art: how learned experience has been tied together in one display and as a result, the emergence of original ideas. It's *all* the art. Everything, as far as I can tell, is doing this all the time. So in that vein, just as we don't expect a long list of references next to every artwork in a gallery, don't expect a long list of references here.

The inspirations that form the spinal cord of this book stem almost exclusively from revelations realised through years of relentless self-inquiry, in the pursuit of the truth of who and what I am. The dialogue between those visions and memories of previous knowledge, is this book. If I had different memories, the dialogue would have been different, but, I believe, the truth that would have sat in dialogue with those memories would have been exactly the same, and that truth is within everyone and everything.

Now, it could be said that I'm using the observations of various experimental results or findings in order to create analogies that fit the concept schema I'm trying to create. That's perfectly reasonable because that's what interpretation is. Whether we interpret observation to fit the narrative of a finite reality made of fundamental objects or as a means to demonstrate the total continuity of the infinity of reality is ultimately up to us. It's also important to note that, although this book is the creation of a concept schema, its intent is to point to something beyond itself. It's not meant to be turned into a monument. It's meant to point in a direction, down a beautiful path, and once you grasp that you are both the destination and the compass, the schema dissolves from view. It is not a lifeboat to cling to for safety, but rather a profound revelation.

I believe that this is the purpose of any concept schema. Like lighthouses, they are supposed to help you avoid misadventure. If you travel *towards* a lighthouse, you're headed for trouble. If you think the lighthouse is beckoning you towards it to discover some kind of treasure, you don't understand the purpose of a lighthouse. Clinging to our concepts of the world and trying to find truth in the concepts themselves, as if the concepts were fundamental, is altogether too literal. It's like investigating the material constitution of the fire in the lighthouse in an attempt to discover the hidden meaning of the lighthouse. The meaning is not *inside* the fire.

In light of that, I encourage you to apply your understanding of the concepts presented here in everyday life and see how you feel. Do you feel more connected? Do you feel more tuned to the environment? Do you feel peaceful? Are your relationships more harmonious and joyful when you apply it? Does any of this stand the test of application? Test it. Use it. Apply it. Then tell me about it. I want to hear about your experience of applying it. Use the email address at the front of the book, whether effective or ineffective, tell me. This is only the beginning.

The real point of writing this book is to lovingly share the nature of my experience in hope that you too will realise and share in the love present at the heart of the self. I have no interest in fame, and this book is published with anonymity in part, for that reason. Another reason for anonymity is because it really doesn't matter to me who said what, it has always been about whether or not the 'what' that is being said makes any sense. Removing the name - and as such any chance of authority - focuses on what is being said, not who is saying it. The focus is the content, not the authority of the author.

In closing, I repeat what I said at the start. I would love for this to be the beginning of a dialogue. Whether you agree or disagree, whether something has upset you or excited you, let's talk. Let's sit peacefully together and discuss the nature of reality.

Only Love.

Always.

O

Milton Keynes UK
Ingram Content Group UK Ltd.
UKHW010700210823
427162UK00004B/96

9 781739 135621